IMAGES OF ILLNESS
SECOND EDITION

IMAGES OF ILLNESS
SECOND EDITION

Linda L. Viney

ROBERT E. KRIEGER PUBLISHING COMPANY
MALABAR, FLORIDA
1989

Original Edition 1983
Second Edition 1989

Printed and Published by
ROBERT E. KRIEGER PUBLISHING CO., INC.
KRIEGER DRIVE
MALABAR, FLORIDA 32950

Library of Congress Cataloging-in-Publication Data

Viney, Linda L.
    Images of illness.

    Bibliography: p.
    Includes index.
    1. Sick--Psychology.   2. Imagery (Psychology)
I.   Title.
R726.5.V55   1989   155.9'16   88-26608
ISBN 0-89464-345-2 (alk. paper)

10   9   8   7   6   5   4   3   2

ACKNOWLEDGEMENTS

Many of my colleagues contributed to this work which has been financed over a number of years by the Australian Research Grants Committee, Australian Institute of Health and the Commonwealth Department of Health. I would like to thank especially Susan Beattie, Yvonne Benjamin, Terry Bunn, Rosemary Caruana, Alex Clarke, Levinia Crooks, Carole Preston and Mary Westbrook. I would also like to thank the research participants, those people who in spite of their pain and discomfort shared their experiences of illness with us. Their privacy has been protected since, while personal names are used in this book, they are never real names. The dignity of these people has, I hope, also been preserved by writing of them not as "patients" but as people with ideas, feelings, attitudes and beliefs like you and me.

PREFACE TO THE SECOND EDITION

Few tasks which psychologists attempt can be as rewarding as revising a book they have written. I certainly enjoyed this particular revision. It gave me a welcome chance to reflect again on the images of illness I had identified, using information from both my continuing research with people who are ill and my colleague's reports of similar work in the literature since the first edition of Images of illness five years ago. My own research since that time has developed to include older people than those who originally participated, as well as those affected by AIDS.

All of this work has confirmed the central message of this book: that people respond, not to their actual illnesses or injuries, but to their images of them, which they themselves create and can therefore change. I hope that Images of illness will continue to be, in its updated form, as useful to people as it has been. Many kind readers have assured me of its value to them, including illness researchers, professional workers with the ill, families and close friends of the ill and, most important to me, ill people themselves.

SECTION 1

FOCUSSING ON IMAGES

Images are the means by which we interpret and make sense of our experiences. They are made up of ideas, feelings, attitudes and beliefs. The first chapter provides a description of the theoretical approach I have taken to peoples' images of illness. The second is about the methods I used to identify these images in the research on which this book is based.

In chapter 1 I deal with the importance of images in peoples' lives. It develops the proposition that the reality we imagine is as important as any physical reality. The role of meaning in the understanding of images is discussed. So, too, is the way in which people build up images on the basis of their experience, so that everyone's personal images of illness are worth exploring. I have provided some examples of images of illness, as well as some information about their meanings. Finally, some of the potential uses of this book are noted. It can help people who are dealing with illness to come to terms with their own illness images. It can help their family and friends to do so. It can also help health care professionals to understand those images and their implications for people who are ill.

In chapter 2 I am concerned with the means by which these private and personal images can be identified. I have examined some of the arguments for and against asking people to report on their experiences of illness. The need to make such a request in the context of an appropriate relationship is acknowledged. My choice of the method of content analysis to identify patterns in their responses is examined. Finally, before some of the images which emerged from the patterns are analysed, the sample of severely ill people who participated in the research is described.

CHAPTER 1

THE IMPORTANCE OF IMAGES

"The events we face today are subject to as
great a variety of constructions as our wits
can contrive." (Kelly, 1970, p. 1)

One important reality is what people imagine it to be. This is as true for people dealing with illness as it is for people dealing with other events. It is the images of illness which people build up which affect how they act when illness becomes an important aspect of their own experience. By "images", I mean their representations of illness-related events which include not only ideas but feelings, attitudes and beliefs. Images involve meanings which people have developed through their efforts to understand what is happening to them. They believe these images to be true reflections of their world. Each person creates unique images which are personal to himself or herself. Yet is is also possible to share the meaning of these images. This book has been written in order to cast light on and share some of our most common images of illness.

This notion that the most important reality may not be the reality of the physical world but the reality which we create when we interpret the information we have about that world is not a new one (Kant, 1781; Brentano, 1874). There is a philosophical approach called phenomenology, the history of which has been well documented (Spiegelberg, 1969), which takes this view. Husserl (1927) developed this notion even further. Not only, he argued, are there always some differences between experienced and physical reality, between my interpretation of my illness and that illness itself. He believed also that the only available knowledge is that constructed by people for themselves. In other words, it is only our images of illness that can be known to us, not the illnesses themselves (Sartre, 1962). We can only understand how people act in relation to illness if we understand their images of it. Imagination is the key to this kind of reality (Kelly, 1969a).

The Meanings of Images

Implicit in this approach is the need to gain access to peoples' images of illness. It favours taking the perspective on illness that ill people take, the perspective of the actor rather than of the observer (Bogdan and Taylor, 1975). It also favours remembering that the perspective of any one ill person is only one of many possible alternative perspectives (Bhaskar, 1975). It follows from this approach that the findings of any one psychologist provide only one image among many possible images and that at all times that image is an interpretation of reality. Some psychologists seek for truth when they carry out their research. Others are not looking for truth but for meaning (Rychlak, 1988). This research is of the latter kind. I know that this book represents my own interpretation of the events I have observed.

Such interpretation becomes meaningful only when there is interaction between the physical event which is observed and the images of which people are aware (Gendlin, 1962). A psychology of illness must therefore consider illness in the context of people's images of illness(Kleinman, 1986). Much psychological research has been based on measurement. There are many advantages to the use of numbers to define the events with which we are dealing. For example, it makes it easy to make comparisons between images of different events or different peoples' images of the same events. Much of the psychological literature referred to in this book is of that kind. However, with this approach, images are our focus of concern. Meaning therefore takes precedence over measurement (Giorgi, 1971). Language becomes important (Gergen, 1985). It is also important that the level of meaning in the images which are under focus is retained and that it is not broken down into units which are too small or out of context (Harré, 1974). In this work sentences are the units of meaning explored and the context to which they refer is described.

The Construction of Images

One of the best accounts of how images are constructed has been provided by Kelly (1955). The act of construction can be seen to take place in the following example (Kockelmans, 1966). When we perceive a house for the first time from the front of it we have a limited amount of information about it. We can then move around it and gain more information from different perspectives. We can develop an image on the basis of any one of these perspectives, but it is usually constructed by an integration of them all. Such an image enables us to create some order that is meaningful and relevant to our needs to understand and anticipate out of the multitude of sensations which bombard us (Landfield and Epting, 1985). An image of illness can be based on one's own single sneeze; but it is much more likely to have been constructed out of a life time's experience of one's own colds, influenza and other related illnesses, their effects on oneself in different situations and the ways in which they changed over time. These images of illness are used not only to interpret one's own sneezes but also to make inferences about the sneezing (or pain or paralysis) of others (Jones and Davis, 1965). People try to make sense of themselves and their world and then act according to the images they have of them (Bruner, 1962). They do not react directly to the physical world but to their interpretations of it (Marias, 1967). Images are constructed out of interactions with reality. People structure their world by impressing their own images on it (Holland, 1970). Illness, then, is actively interpreted in terms of the images of illness which we have available to us. Many of them are negative images, with disturbing and disagreeable implications. Some are positive images, with more encouraging and rewarding implications.

Fortunately, our acts of construction are not so rigid as to rule out choices between one kind of image or another. People can be flexible in their construction of images of illness. Each of us exists within a protective covering of our own images (Gordon, 1972). Their construction is a unique process for each individual (Bannister and Fransella, 1986; Strosahl and Ascough, 1981). This is because it is based on the images already available to each individual which are a result of his or her attempts to make sense of earlier experiences. Adults experiencing illness tend to apply to it the images of illness they developed during childhood (Kelly, 1955). Each person has an individual theory of illness which can be studied (Harré, 1974). This is not to say, however, that all images of illness are totally different for each person. Many of our early experiences, especially of illness, have been very similar, resulting in similar images. It is therefore worthwhile searching for some shared images of illness (Hetherington, 1984; Latour and Woolgar, 1979). Particular kinds of illness, because they decrease the likelihood of certain events occurring and increase the likelihood of others, lead to common images. People who cannot walk, for example, do not experience much mobility but they all experience dependence on others. It is also worthwhile, then, to search for images common to certain kinds of illness.

Despite the uniqueness of the construction process, people are able to share images. If communication using images was not possible, then my words would not be making any sense to you now. It is only, however, as one person understands some of the meanings of another's images and that understanding is reciprocated, that meaningful communication can occur (Kelly, 1955; Schütz, 1967). It is only as I understand something of your purpose, as someone who is ill, a friend or relative of an ill person, or a health care giver, in reading this book, and you understand something of my purpose in writing it, that we can communicate. It is through communication that we construct many of our images. The meaning of a communicated message can be found in the change which it produces in the image of a listener (Boulding, 1956). A reality is constructed which is neither the reality of the physical world nor that of the individual, but a social reality which is shared by communities and cultures (Berger and Luckman, 1972). Images of illness have been constructed in our Western culture which influence greatly the ways in which we interpret and so react to different types of illness.

Some Images of Illness

Images of cancer have become powerful social realities in our society. A comparison of these cancer images with those of the disease which was most frightening to our grand-parents and great-grand-parents in the nineteenth century - tuberculosis - is interesting (Sontag, 1977). Of course, none of these images was or is necessarily an accurate representation of the disease in question. Tuberculosis was said to be a disease of the poor; while cancer is said to be prevalent in the wealthier middle classes. Tuberculosis was seen as painless; cancer is seen as painful. Tuberculosis was romantasized in novels as an aphrodisiac; cancer is written of as desexualizing. Even the images for the treatment of the two diseases have been constructed differently: people with tuberculosis were wooed and coaxed while people with cancer are assaulted with almost military force (they have been "attacked" by cancer and there is talk of "invasion" by cancer cells and "bombardment" of the cells). These images are very vivid.

Culturally shared images of illness are very powerful (Duval, 1984). This power comes, in part, from language in which they are expressed. When we talk about illness, we choose, for example, to use nouns rather than verbs to describe it. Talking about "my cancer" and "my husband's heart condition" leads us to think of them as passive entities and not as part of our active, functioning body. We also think of them as separate and not as part of our whole. This language has moulded our experience of illness so that is has become a thing, rigidly defined and unchanging (Warner, 1976-77). Illness and disability have been simplified by this conceptualization to something concrete and influenced by only one set of factors, physical factors. If our cultural view of them were couched in the language of action as interference with ongoing function, we might be less prone to use surgery unnecessarily and more open to the role played in the development of and recovery from illness by psychological and social factors.

As well as these culturally shared images, there are illness images which are constructed by individuals when faced with personal illness. It has been established that severely ill people often put so much of their reduced energy into making sense of what is happening to them, for example, into attributing blame so as to retain their own belief system, that medical help is not sought until this feat is accomplished (Janis and Rodin, 1979). It has also been observed that when the symptoms of an illness are clear and catastrophic - as with a heart attack - the sufferer works long and hard to make sense of them

(Cowie, 1975; Thurer, Levine and Thurer, 1980-81; Egger and Stix, 1984). She, or more likely he, will compare his attack-related symptoms with those of his other health problems (comparing them, for example, with those of indigestion). He also will compare them with symptoms reported by others who have also suffered heart attacks ("Yes, I had a pain in my shoulder too"). It seems that this is a way of building up enough information to be able to make predictions about similar symptoms in the future.

People with severe illnesses other than heart disease also search for meaning in what is happening to them (Mechanic, 1974). Sometimes they search for it in those shared images which are constructed within cultures. In our culture these images include interpretations of illness as the enemy, as punishment for some wickedness or as a personal weakness for which blame may be laid (Lipowski, 1970; Blumberg, Flaherty and Lewis, 1980). Yet it is also possible in our culture to view illness as a challenge. People expand their images of their illness by searching out causes for it (Koslowsky, Kroog and La Voie, 1978). ("Did I have my heart attack because I had too much tension at work or because I smoked too much?"). Whatever images of it they develop, these images affect the ways in which people adapt to their illness (Mechanic, 1977). For example, people who have become paraplegics or quadraplegics through accidents may come to cope better with their disability if they can accept some of their own responsibility for the accident (Bulman and Wortman, 1977).

Images can be developed and expanded in this way in response to illness and injury. They can also be constricted. This usually occurs when a person is threatened by events. A person who has recently been hospitalized with a severe illness, for example, is subject to considerate threat because so much of what he or she is experiencing is new and unpleasant (Kornfield, 1972; Kinsman et al ., 1976; Volicer, 1978). She is likely to be weak and in pain, dependent on strangers, isolated from those close to her and confused by the as yet unknown procedures and events in which she has to participate. It is little wonder that, in such circumstances, her world "shrinks" to include just herself and to the hospital ward (Cassell, 1976). Dealing with a smaller world can help her to get a better grip on it. Reduced complexity reduces confusion.

A similar constriction of images is experienced by people mourning the loss of their old life style through illness (Woodfield and Viney, 1985). This, too, is a response to failure to make sense of what is happening. However, images are important to any psychological study of illness for yet another reason. Having a flexible and useful set of images may protect one from illness. Images which bring to people a stable and pervasive confidence that events are predictable and will end in the best possible way seem to gain this protective effect (Antonovsky, 1979). Whether this sense of confidence is based on a belief in oneself, other people or a supernatural being makes no difference. Of course, it is not only images of illness which contribute to this sense of confidence but images of events not related to illness as well.

Some Meanings of Images of Illness

During this decade more attention has been paid to peoples' images of illness. For example, researchers have tried to experience what it is like to have the symptoms of certain illnesses and how to construct one's own images of them (Bernal, 1984). They have come to recognize that we build these images out of our ordinary, everyday experiences and not out of specialist medical experience (Gannick and Jesperson, 1984), and that they stem from beliefs about links between symptom and disease which people held long before their current symptoms became apparent (Bishop and Converse, 1986). A team of researchers which has been working on these images for almost two decades describes them as common sense models of illness (Leventhal, Merenz and Steele, 1982). They have found four factors to be important to the development of these illness images (Leventhal, Meyer and Nerenz, 1980). The first of these factors is made up of the identifying characteristics of the illness, such as the location of the symptoms, how they are felt and seen, how long they last and the language with which they are expressed. The other factors that they consider influence the development of images are perceptions of the causes of the illness, its course over time and its likely outcomes.

Images of illness can be said to have meanings that are shared between people who are ill if their emotional reactions to illness can be used as evidence for this statement (Viney, in pressa). There are even special meanings that are shared by people who are close to death

(Viney and Westbrook, 1986-87). Many of the same dimensions of meaning are used in peoples' images of illness and health (Millstein and Irwin, 1987). One of the differences between these two types of images concerns ability to function well. In images of illness general functioning is involved, but images of health are more specifically concerned with filling roles already established at work or with family and friends. Not all illness-related meanings are shared, however. Just as there is evidence that people change the images they use in coping with life as they enter different stages of the life span (Viney, 1987a), there is also evidence that images of illness change at different stages of that span (Prohaska et al., 1987; Viney and Westbrook, 1985; Westbrook and Viney, 1983).

Another recent exploration of the meanings of images of illness has arisen from attribution theory. This psychological theory suggests that people account for their experiences of events by attributing causes to them (Antaki and Brewin, 1981; Harvey and Weary, 1985; Weiner, 1985). People with cancer, for example, have been shown to make some important attributions about its causes (Baider and Sarell, 1983), as have people with rheumatoid arthritis (Affleck et al., 1987), cardiac conditions (Affleck et al., 1987) and AIDS (Acquired Immune Deficiency Syndrome) (Moulton et al., 1987). The major attributions which have been studied are internal (self taking responsibility) and external (responsibility given to other people or events). In most hospitals, consulting rooms and surgeries the dominant images of illness held by patients and health professionals alike tend to have external attributions for both the causes of illnesses and their treatment (Brickman, et al., 1982). This can mean that patients have to contend with many overwhelming helpless and depressed images (Brickman, et al., 1983). However, since illness itself is an unwelcome event, images of it which contain these external attributions may lead to better illness outcomes (Burish, et al., 1984; Firth-Cozens and Brewin, in press; Peterson and Seligman, 1987); and attribution therapy is available if needed (Layden, 1982).

Images of illness, having a powerful impact on peoples' personal experience, are likely to have such an influence on their interpersonal experiences as well. People who are ill communicate their images to a set of interacting but separate social systems made up of the professional staff who deal with them, their family, close friends and their community (Viney, Clarke and Benjamin, 1986). While some of these images are shared with their family and community, sharing them with professional staff is more difficult. Indeed, the impact of professional training has been to replace "common sense" images of illness with professional ones. This training enables professionals to do much for patients that patients cannot do for themselves, but it does make sharing of images of illness between patients and staff difficult. There is an increasing concern with helping health professionals to understand and work with the images of their patients, especially physicians, who seem to be the most distanced from them by their training (Evans et al., 1986; Linden, 1985; Williams and Wood, 1986).

The Importance of Images

In this chapter I have proposed that people's images of reality are important for a psychological study of illness. I have described some of the implications of my approach and traced something of its history. I have also emphasized the importance of personal meanings to this study. The construction of images has been explored, together with the unique nature of that construction process and the shared or common images which stem from it. Finally, some illness images have been examined.

It is now apparent why I have been at pains to describe my own psychology of illness. It is characteristic of my approach that its assumptions are made as explicit as possible (Giorgi, 1985; Barton and Maes, 1983). Without this sharing of assumptions, as I noted earlier, communication cannot take place. Any view which has its focus on people's construction of images cannot fail to take into account the researcher's own images (Giddens, 1976). It must therefore be reflexive, that is, it must use the same approach to account for the researcher as for the researched (Kelly, 1965; Bannister, 1970). This account of illness, then, must reflect my images at least as much as it does those of the ill people we interviewed (Manicas and Secord, 1982; Scarr, 1985). It is with my words that it is written.

This is not an apology for my research, since all research must be dominated by the images of the people who carry it out. Indeed, I believe that this research has helped to extend our understanding of the psychology of illness. It makes apparent, for example, the richness and complexity of some of our images of illness. It identifies some of the shared images which abound in our culture and, at the same time, makes a variety of different perspectives on illness known to us. Finally, it provides evidence of the dynamic interplay between people and their worlds in which images of illness are constructed, elaborated, expanded and constricted (Speigelberg, 1970). Understanding of these images will lead to a better understanding of the interplay of psychological and physical factors in illness (Alexander and French, 1948; Lipowski, Lipsitt and Whybrow, 1977; Gottschalk, 1978). It has been said that psychological research should be evaluated in terms of whether it casts light on common images of the phenomenon studied (Allport, 1955; Hudson, 1972). By this criterion, this research has value.

It also has therapeutic value (Viney, in pressa; Viney & Benjamin, 1983). We are only beginning to learn how to deal psychotherapeutically with people who are experiencing severe illness (Gruen, 1975; Hackett and Cassem, 1975; Cummings and Vandenbos, 1979). We have some evidence that good psychological functioning is linked with good physical functioning (Greer and Watson, 1987; Luborsky and McClellan, 1980-81). Ill people are people who are required to make major changes in their lives. The crisis brought about by these changes may result in poorer coping by patients but it may also result in more flexible, resourceful and enjoyable acting and reacting than they have achieved before (Viney, 1976). One way to achieve this preferred outcome is to highlight the images which patients have constructed; so that they can use them to aid in their own decision making (Epting, 1984). Indeed, to become aware of how we make up our images and of the gap between image and reality, is a helpful step in itself (Mancuso, 1979). People who are ill need not be overwhelmed by their images of illness, if they are aware of their own role in constructing them (Kelly, 1969b). Many forms of therapy can help with this awareness (Neimeyer G.J., 1987). To know that one chooses the world in which one lives is to control it.

CHAPTER 2

IDENTIFYING IMAGES OF ILLNESS

> "I do not see why the report of a person on his
> own mind should not be as intelligible and
> trustworthy as that of a traveller upon a new
> country whose landscapes and inhabitants are of
> a different type to any we ourselves have seen."
>
> (Galton, 1889, p. 21)

Research has been described as a search for patterns (Rogers, 1968; Agnew and Pyke, 1969). This view of the activities of the researcher fits well with the approach I have described in Chapter 1, because it emphasizes his or her role as an active maker of images. It is the researcher who describes the patterns observed, who makes sense of them and who communicates their meaning to others. This last step is a very important one; because it is only when agreement on common meanings by different researchers is possible that the results of research become of value (Popper, 1959). In this book I have focussed on the meanings of peoples' images of illness. Elsewhere I have provided a model of psychological reaction to illness based on them (Viney, 1986a), a review of the measurement-based research that supports that model (Viney, in pressa) and a case study of a women with a cardiac condition in which the powerful interactive effects of these images can be seen (Viney, 1987d).

In order to take our first step, our research team needed to find a way to identify the images of illness which ill people use which was compatible with our theoretical framework (Unger, 1983). Then we to us. In other words, the application of the scientific criterion of interpersonal agreement goes some way to answering that criticism. So long as this research confines itself to dealing, not with the inaccessible images of ill people, but with those which form part of a shared, social reality, it can employ this method effectively (Viney, 1987b). Similarly, the second criticism does not prejudice this research technique so long as I, the researcher, limit what I conclude from it. For me to draw inferences about images of illness of which people were not aware would be to go beyond that limit.

It seems appropriate, then, to take up the view of people, from Chapter 1, as active image-makers and to acknowledge that self-reports will effectively tap into their images (Viney, in pressb). Constructors of images have the power to know and can report that knowledge (Shlien, 1963). They are continually making reports which are relevant to the study of images. I agree with other psychologists (Harré and Secord, 1972) who say of research participants: "Why not ask them?" Three questions, then, remain to be answered. In what context did we ask them, how did we deal with their answers and whom did we ask?

The Context of the Research

Adler, one of the first psychologists to accept the view of people I have described, recommended that the over-riding goal of researchers should be to attain understanding. That understanding was to be gained through empathy (Ansbacher and Ansbacher, 1956). By

"I do not see why the report of a person on his

own mind should not be as intelligible and

trustworthy as that of a traveller upon a new

country whose landscapes and inhabitants are of

a different type to any we ourselves have seen."

(Galton, 1889, p. 21)

Research has been described as a search for patterns (Rogers, 1968; Agnew and Pyke, 1969). This view of the activities of the researcher fits well with the approach I have described in Chapter 1, because it emphasizes his or her role as an active maker of images. It is the researcher who describes the patterns observed, who makes sense of them and who communicates their meaning to others. This last step is a very important one; because it is only when agreement on common meanings by different researchers is possible that the results of research become of value (Popper, 1959). In this book I have focussed on the meanings of peoples' images of illness. Elsewhere I have provided a model of psychological reaction to illness based on them (Viney, 1986a), a review of the measurement-based research that supports that model (Viney, in pressa) and a case study of a women with a cardiac condition in which the powerful interactive effects of these images can be seen (Viney, 1987d).

In order to take our first step, our research team needed to find a way to identify the images of illness which ill people use which was compatible with our theoretical framework (Unger, 1983). Then we could examine their meanings. This was achieved by participating with people in their imagined reality (Bodgan and Taylor,1975). We met with people at their hospital beds, at rehabilitation centres, or at a home, and asked them to share with us their experiences (Glaser and Strauss, 1967). We then described some aspects of their experience, using their own words to generate our descriptions. We were concerned with description rather than identifying causes and effects (Giorgi, 1985). We therefore dealt with words rather than numbers (Kohler, 1938).

The kinds of people we approached, the question we asked and the contexts in which we asked them are detailed later in this chapter. However, certain issues which influenced our decisions about these steps merit some thought before these details are described. These issues can be considered in the form of questions we posed to ourselves about our methods. Was it appropriate for us to ask people about their images of illness and, if so, how could we do so? What was the most fruitful context for doing so? And what could we do to communicate their answers to others? These questions will now be considered.

Asking For Personal Reports

Researchers other than psychologists (for example, physicists) have long recognized the appropriateness of relying on personal reports about images (Bridgman, 1959; McKellar, 1962). Psychologists have, however, been very wary of this simple method

(Boring, 1953). Some have claimed that personal reports are too vague and inaccurate to be useful, and even that they may produce artifactual "memories" which have been constructed only in retrospect (Cohen and Lazarus, 1973). This seems unlikely to be a problem for the eliciting of images of illness, because studies have shown that events which have been accompanied by strong emotions are more often remembered than those not accompanied by such emotions (Casey, Masuda and Holmes, 1967; Bryant and Trockel, 1976). Illness does, of course, arouse strong emotions. The other reason why this criticism does not create a problem for this research is that it has not been a retrospective study, relying on memories. We interviewed all our informants while they were ill. Memories did, however, emerge as they shared their images with us. It is therefore useful to know, from other independent research, that such memories were likely to be those contributing to or illuminated by the images with which they were currently dealing (Bower, 1981).

Two other criticisms of the method of asking people to report on their own images remain to be considered. One is that no independent assessment of the accuracy of self-reports is possible (Beloff, 1973). The other is that self-report is not possible when the informant is not aware of the phenomenon which he or she is asked to describe (Bakan, 1967). As to the first criticism, it is true that I cannot guarantee that the image you present to me is an accurate representation of the one you have in your head, any more than you can guarantee the same for me. However, if we can agree on an image, then it is of use to us. In other words, the application of the scientific criterion of interpersonal agreement goes some way to answering that criticism. So long as this research confines itself to dealing, not with the inaccessible images of ill people, but with those which form part of a shared, social reality, it can employ this method effectively (Viney, 1987b). Similarly, the second criticism does not prejudice this research technique so long as I, the researcher, limit what I conclude from it. For me to draw inferences about images of illness of which people were not aware would be to go beyond that limit.

It seems appropriate, then, to take up the view of people, from Chapter 1, as active image-makers and to acknowledge that self-reports will effectively tap into their images (Viney, in pressb). Constructors of images have the power to know and can report that knowledge (Shlien, 1963). They are continually making reports which are relevant to the study of images. I agree with other psychologists (Harré and Secord, 1972) who say of research participants: "Why not ask them?" Three questions, then, remain to be answered. In what context did we ask them, how did we deal with their answers and whom did we ask?

The Context of the Research

Adler, one of the first psychologists to accept the view of people I have described, recommended that the over-riding goal of researchers should be to attain understanding. That understanding was to be gained through empathy (Ansbacher and Ansbacher, 1956). By empathy, he meant a comprehending of someone else from within their own frame of reference. Empathy refers to meanings - ideational, emotional, attitudinal and belief-related meanings. This empathic approach can be seen as a form of listening (Keen, 1975) or attending to verbal and tonal patterns so as to establish meanings. Such empathic listening is only possible if the relationship between speaker and listener is comfortable for both of them.

The context in which the research question was to be asked, then, had to be a relationship which was valued by both researcher and informant. Some kind of interaction was necessary. Without interaction no information could be exchanged. That interaction needed to take place so that a relationship was formed. This was important for the research participant who might not trust his or her researcher sufficiently to disclose private images without it (Wortman et al., 1980). It was also considered to be important for the researchers who would not be able to listen well without it (Mair, 1970). An encounter was therefore arranged through which meaningful exchanges could take place (Armistead, 1974). This technique has been used successfully in the original investigations of childrens' developing images of the world (Piaget, 1930).

Perhaps the most important aspect of this relationship was the role of co-researcher or informed collaborator to which the ill people were introduced (Viney, 1987c). It has been used to some extent in other research (Fischer, W. 1974), but has been best described as a new role for the clients of professional psychologists (Fischer, C.T.

1985). To help our research participants take on this role, they were fully appraised of the goals of the research and their help enlisted to achieve them. They were also fully informed about the methods being used to do so and asked to use these methods in the best way they could. In other words, we told our research participants of our interest in people's images of illness and asked to help us describe them accurately by talking freely of their illness experiences. We believe that in most instances they were able to do this, especially when they became aware of and accepted our empathic listening to them.

Content Analysis: A Way of Listening

Content analysis is the method of listening which we used to organize and interpret the answers of our research participants (Viney, 1983c). It enabled us to identify patterns in what they told us which, in time, resolved into images. It can be applied to any account of events that is expressed in words, since it involves the searching of the verbal content for certain kinds of themes. As it was applied to the relatively free and unstructured responses of ill people to an open-ended question about their illness, it had certain advantages. It enabled them to describe their unique images without undue interference from our research team. It was better than asking directly for reports of their images, about which many people were likely to be ambivalent and therefore cautious in revealing them. It provided what was essentially a psychological trace of those images, just as biochemical analyses of body products reveal traces of physiological activity (Westbrook and

Viney, 1977). It was not situation-specific in the way that other assessment techniques, such as questionnaires and check lists are, and it provided the multiple perspectives on the images of illness which were needed (Viney, 1980).

The themes to be analysed had been defined in a set of content analysis scales which was applied to the responses. Some of these scales had been developed for other purposes in the United States (Gottschalk, 1979; Gottschalk and Gleser, 1969; Gottschalk, Winget and Gleser, 1969), but these had been shown to be effective with Australian informants (Viney and Manton, 1974). Others (Viney and Westbrook, 1976; 1979; Westbrook, 1976; Westbrook and Viney, 1980) have been developed more recently for this work. These themes included the distressing images of uncertainty, as identified in the scoring criteria for the Cognitive Anxiety Scale, (Viney and Westbrook, 1976), anxiety-laden images (the Total Anxiety Scale, Gottschalk and Gleser, 1969; Gottschalk, Winget and Gleser, 1969), anger-laden images (the Hostility Out and Ambivalent Hostility Scales, Gottschalk and Gleser, 1969; Gottschalk, Winget and Gleser, 1969), images of helplessness (the Pawn Scale, Westbrook and Viney, 1980), depression-laden images (the Hostility In Scale, Gottschalk and Gleser, 1969; Gottschalk, Winget and Gleser, 1969) and images of isolation (the Separation Anxiety Scale, Gottschalk and Gleser, 1969; Gottschalk, Winget and Gleser, 1969). They also included more welcome images such as happy ones (as defined by the scoring criteria for the Positive Affect Scale, Westbrook, 1976), images of competence (the Origin Scale, Westbrook and Viney, 1980) and images involving family and friends (the Sociality Scale, Viney and Westbrook, 1979). Considerable evidence is available that each of these scales measures the type of images it claims to measure (Gottschalk, Lolas and Viney, 1986). Each of them has also demonstrated sufficient agreement between panels of researchers working independently to lay claim to a high level of interjudge reliability (Viney, 1983c). The images to which they refer, then, are shared by a number of people and are unique neither to the designers of the scales nor to the informants.

There were other reasons why we chose to deal with the responses of participants in the research to a direct but open-ended question using these content analysis scales. It was not because they provided a way of translating meaning into numbers, thereby enabling effective statistical comparisons of people and events. The work in which we used them for those purposes has been reported elsewhere (Viney and Westbrook, 1981a,b; 1982a,b,c; 1985;1986; Westbrook and Viney, 1981; 1982; 1983). It was rather that they make explicit the propositions on which we, the researchers, were relying rather than having them influence and possibly bias the research in unknown ways (Viney, 1981b; 1982, 1987b). Also, they make rigourous and replicable access to the experience of others possible to an extent that no other approach known to us does; and they tap into that experience as it changes over time. Finally, these content analysis scales provide indicators of the quality of life which ill people experience (Viney and

Westbrook, 1981b).

The content analysis procedure we used was as follows. The oral responses of our research participants to an open-ended question were, with their permission, recorded and transcribed. These responses were then divided into units, each of which contained an active verb. The resulting clauses were searched for the themes which were of interest during each search. For example, when listening for images of competence, themes showing intention, effort and ability, together with acting on one's world and being a creative source were recorded, in accordance with the scoring criteria of the Origin Scale (Westbrook and Viney, 1980). Evidence of the interjudge reliability of our procedure has been reported elsewhere (Viney, Benjamin and Preston, in pressd; Viney et al., 1985b; Viney and Westbrook, 1981a). This was the question we asked:

> "I'd like you to talk for a few minutes about your life at the moment - the good things and the bad - what it is like for you".

The Participants in the Research

In order to gain access to images of illness it was necessary to decide how we would approach people, in what context we would do so and how we would deal with their response to that approach. We decided to ask ill people directly about their experiences of illness, to do so in the context of a relationship which encouraged them to take the role of the informed collaborator and to apply content analysis to organize and make sense of their answers. It now remains to describe the ill people to whom it was posed.

Our question was asked as part of a dialogue between one of eight trained interviewers and each informant. Many of the informants participated in this dialogue during hospitalization, either for acute illness or injury or for a flare-up of some chronic condition. Others were approached during one of their regular visits to a rehabilitation centre or through a support group. A few more were seen at home since their illness prevented even that kind of outing. Because there is some evidence that people react differently to illness according to whether they are hospitalized or at home (Viney and Westbrook, 1981a; 1982c; 1984), we tried to follow up the first two groups at home to get their responses to the same question. We have been successful with about 65% of our original participants.

Some 800 people coping with illness in Australia have participated in this research. The number of men and women involved has been similar. This is appropriate because, although in Western cultures more women than men receive medical treatment (Cleary, Mechanic and Greenley, 1982), more men are hospitalized with chronic life threatening problems such as heart attacks and strokes (Mechanic, 1978). Their ages ranged from 18 to 95 years, with the majority being in their fifties, sixties and seventies. Three quarters of them were married and most of those had children. In terms of education, some of them had only completed primary school. Others had reached mid-high school, yet others had completed high school, and a small proportion had tertiary qualifications. They represented the full range of educational attainment. They also represented the full range of socioeconomic circumstances (Congalton,1969).

All of these people were dealing with the threat of severe and often painful illness or the disabling effects of accidents. Many of those with acute illness were scheduled for exploratory or corrective surgery for problems such as back pain and gastro-intestinal difficulties. Both men and women were hospitalized for surgery for genito-urinary malfunctions. There was also a number who were hospitalized for observation and hospital care for respiratory problems, such as asthma and pneumonia, and for gastro-intestinal problems, such as ulcers. People were seen as dealing with chronic illness if they had a condition which would last at least six months or had caused a permanent disability (Australian Bureau of Statistics, 1979). The largest group of people in this category were those who had had heart attacks (myocardial infarctions) or suffered from other heart syndromes, such as angina. Victims of strokes (cerebrovascular accidents) were common. There were, too, people with specific disorders, such as diabetes, and progressive diseases of the nervous system, such as multiple sclerosis. Paraplegics and quadriplegics - victims of accidents - shared their experiences with us. We also included people with cancer and AIDS as suffering form chronic disease. Even people whose symptoms of these diseases have been in remission for months or years, we found, are dealing with persistent threat and will continue to do so.

It would seem that, with information from people with such a variety of body damage with which to deal and of futures to look forward to, a range of images specific to certain illnesses would have resulted. This did not prove to be the case. As we "listened" with our content analysis to their accounts of their experiences, we found certain patterns or themes emerging which transcended these illness groups and were common to many ill and injured people. These patterns resolved into images of illness. Many of these images are distressing and inhibiting ones. These images, what is known about them, and how they can be coped with, I examine in Section 2 of this book. The more enjoyable and facilitating images, their implications and how they can be encouraged, I describe in Section 3.

SECTION 2

DISTRESSING IMAGES OF ILLNESS

In Section 2 six types of images of illness which have predominantly distressing effects on peoples' lives are introduced. They are described in terms of the emotions which dominate them: uncertainty, anxiety, anger, helplessness, depression and isolation. In each chapter I deal with a different type of image, using the same format. In the introductory section the ways in which people express these images are considered. The ill people speak for themselves. A review of the psychological and psychiatric literatures follows, in which what has been established about the implications of the images is examined. Each chapter concludes with some suggestions about how to cope with the images. These suggestions are based on the proposition, put forward in Chapter 1, that people need not be overwhelmed by the disturbing emotions which are associated with these images of illness if they recognize that they, themselves, have developed them and so can influence and control them.

CHAPTER 3

IMAGES OF UNCERTAINTY

"So much unnecessary trauma was caused by my ignorance."

(John J., cardiac condition)

One image of uncertainty which many people report has to do with the lack of information available to them about their illness. "THERE'S A LOT I DON'T KNOW ABOUT MY ILLNESS" is one of the forms in which this image is expressed. This has been said about cancer, heart attacks, strokes, multiple sclerosis, AIDS, and diabetes and, in fact, most of the disease with which our informants have been dealing. Some of the speakers mean that they know little about their own illness and the course it might take. Others are protesting that health care professionals have not told them more about it. Yet others are commenting on the lack of knowledge about it in our culture, about its symptoms, its treatment and its outcomes. Whichever meanings are intended, however, all of the people who make such a statement are experiencing uncertainty. Uncertainty is often an appropriate reaction to illness or injury. It is true that we have little cultural knowledge about many diseases. It is true that many health care professionals do not fully inform people about their illnesses. It is also true that the course of many diseases for any one individual cannot be predicted accurately.

Uncertainty, paradoxically, may be reality-based. This is especially so during the early stages of illness or immediately after accidents causing severe injury. Both kinds of events can provoke a crisis for people (Viney and Benjamin, 1983). A crisis is a time of emotional disruption (Caplan, 1964); but it is also a time of disruption of people's usual ways of interpreting events. Their images of reality are disrupted (Parkes, 1971). Without their old images, people are at a loss, that is, uncertain. Resolution of their crisis can only be achieved when they reassert their cognitive grip on events (Katz et al ., 1970; Taplin, 1971).

"WHY HAS THIS HAPPENED TO ME?" is a question often asked by people who have recently discovered that they are ill. They ask it of themselves, of health care professionals and even of friends and relatives. It represents something of the confusion they feel that, having at last as adults worked out who they are and where they are going in life, they are suddenly faced with an aspect of themselves with which they have not had many dealings and a future which is now in doubt. Their senses of identity and of continuity are threatened. Only very few of the people who were severely ill or injured, who spoke with us, have not been troubled by this question. One was an elderly widow, with a strong and sustaining belief in God. Her surgeon, doing exploratory surgery for cancer, who was all too used to the question said to her: "I suppose you are going to say, why me?". She answered calmly: "As a Christian, I would say, why not me?". Her sense of identity, and the promise of continuity which her faith provided, protected her from the illness-related uncertainty which most people experience. She did not need to alter in any way these images which were so important to her.

This chapter deals with uncertainty-laden images. It follows the plan I have outlined. First, some examples of such images (Viney and Westbrook, 1976) are described. They include the shock of being told of one's physical state, uncertainty about the illness and its treatment, and concerns about the future and about others' reaction to oneself. Some of their own uncertainty which ill people see reflected in others is also described. Second, some of the implications of images of uncertainty are examined. Researchers have long been aware of illness-associated uncertainty; and their findings concerning it are of interest. Third, how ill and injured people can learn to cope with uncertainty is also discussed. With this goal in mind, the importance of working with the images which people are using to make sense of events is emphasized, and some of the effects of crisis counselling are elaborated. A brief dialogue from such counselling, focussing on a man's entry to hospital, is provided. The importance of preparation for surgery is also considered, as is the decision-making role of people who are hospitalized.

Some Illness-Related Images of Uncertainty

As has been observed, the initial shock of finding out about the severity of an illness and of sudden hospitalization can give rise to many uncertainty-laden images. "I DIDN'T KNOW THERE WAS

ANYTHING WRONG WITH ME" reflects the disbelief which this speaker was still experiencing, as does this statement: "I CAN'T BELIEVE THAT IT COULD BE ME THAT IS SO ILL." "IT ALL HAPPENED SO FAST" shows a confusion probably brought about, not just by the speed of the illness-related events experienced, but by their variety and strangeness. Some people have been confused in this way by the multitude of implications of the information they have been given: "WHEN YOU ARE FIRST TOLD ABOUT MASTECTOMY, IT'S NOT THE LOSS OF THE BREAST BUT THE NAME... CANCER... THAT SHOCKS YOU." Being hospitalized, too, can add to the shocks. "COMING TO HOSPITAL WAS A BIT OF A SURPRISE." "I DIDN'T KNOW WHAT TO DO WHEN I WENT IN AT FIRST. EVERYONE SEEMED TO KNOW WHAT WAS GOING ON EXCEPT ME."

Uncertainty can also be generated by the actual illness or injury with which people are dealing. Often the shock element continues. "IT'S A SHOCK TO YOU, TO KNOW YOU'RE A DIABETIC." "THE BAD THING IS THE SHOCK OF LOSING THE LEG." "BEING A VERY ACTIVE PERSON, THIS WAS A BIT OF A SHOCK TO ME." And it is often followed by difficulties in adjustment to the new body state and life style: "IT WAS HARD TO GET USED TO AT FIRST." Not being well informed about the symptoms does not help: "I DIDN'T KNOW WHAT IT ALL MEANT." Uncertainty can grow like this, whether because of poor communication with health care professionals, "THE DOCTOR DIDN'T EXPLAIN MUCH ABOUT MY ILLNESS", or because of lack of knowledge on everyone's part, "MY HEALTH PROBLEM IS A LOT

WORSE THAN WE EXPECTED."

Uncertainty-laden images are also constructed when people do not understand their own reactions to their illness, as in these examples: "FOR NO REASON AT ALL I'LL BE VERY DEPRESSED AND THEN SUDDENLY SNAP OUT OF IT" and "I WAS GETTING VERY TIRED AND CRANKY: AND I DIDN'T REALISE WHY." If uncertainty is often generated by illness and injury it is also generated by many of the treatments of them. As one woman with cancer, who was trying to prepare for a form of therapy which was new to her, said: "RADIOTHERAPY IS HARD TO FACE. IT'S FACING THE UNKNOWN." She was able to deal with it much better after she had been assured by another patient in the waiting room that the treatment machine would not actually touch her. Even unexpected recovery can be alarming, "ALL OF A SUDDEN I CAME GOOD AGAIN"; especially if no-one knows why and so cannot reproduce the miracle if and when it is needed again. But it has been surgery which has stimulated the most uncertainty laden images for the people we have interviewed. "I HAVEN'T HAD A BIG OPERATION BEFORE. I HAVEN'T A CLUE HOW I'LL FEEL AFTERWARDS." "ITS BEEN A BIT OF A SHOCK, HAVING THIS OPERATION." "I WASN'T REALLY PREPARED FOR THE HYSTERECTOMY." As we shall see later, preparation of people for surgery enables them to deal better with it.

As soon as people become severely ill or injured their future becomes clouded. They cannot make plans for coming events with the certainty they used to; and the plans they have already made are often disrupted. Some illnesses entail a future which is especially difficult to predict: "IT'S THE TYPE OF DISEASE WHERE YOU WON'T KNOW HOW IT'S GOING TO HIT YOU." Some severe illnesses and injuries also make major changes in life style necessary: "I'VE BEEN USED TO WORKING HARD ALL MY LIFE. NOW..." Even those people whose treatment has been successful have momentarily glimpsed those uncertainties of the future: "IF THE OPERATION HAD NOT BEEN A SUCCESS I DON'T KNOW WHAT I WOULD HAVE DONE." Even planning realistically for the future can be difficult. An elderly man who was being encouraged by health professionals to "cope" better with the effects of his heart condition serves as an example. As he said: "'COPE' IS A NEW FASHIONED WORD. WHEN I WAS YOUNG, I WAS TAUGHT TO ACCEPT WHAT HAPPENED, NOT TO 'COPE' WITH IT." While able to use his own images to prepare for his future, he was not able to use those from other people which were alien to him.

Because one's own images of illness may differ from those of others, it can be difficult to understand their reactions to oneself when ill. As a gentleman of the same vintage as the one already described remarked: "THINGS AREN'T AS THEY WERE WHEN I WAS A YOUNG MAN IN SCOTLAND." Not only things and places have changed, but people too. And it is not only age which can be a barrier to sharing images and so to communication. Other barriers are set up, often by fear. As many of our informants noted, people sometimes vanish quickly rather than have to respond to someone who is severely ill or injured: "YOU THINK YOU'VE GOT FRIENDS. THEN ALL OF A SUDDEN YOU DON'T HAVE ANY ANY MORE." This communication problem often extends to relatives too: "THE CHILDREN AREN'T COMING TO SEE ME HERE. I DON'T KNOW WHY." And it can also occur for ill people trying to communicate with them, especially about their illness. This is the subject which is most important to them but about which they may have little information. One of the questions often asked of physicians discussing major health problems, regardless of what they are, is "WHAT AM I GOING TO TELL MY HUSBAND (WIFE) ABOUT IT?"

Of course other people may be just as uncertain as the ill person. Ill people are aware of this, whether it be in health professionals, "THEY CAN'T FIND ANYTHING WRONG WITH MY LEG", family and friends, "NO ONE ELSE KNOWS WHAT IT'S LIKE TO BE IN A WHEELCHAIR", or the general public "FEW PEOPLE KNOW ANYTHING ABOUT EMPHYSEMA." And it is not only the diseases and treatments which they see as not being understood by others, but people's reactions to them as well. "ALL MY CHILDREN WILL TELL YOU THAT I HAVE HAD A COMPLETE PERSONALITY CHANGE SINCE THE ILLNESS", said one woman with diabetes who saw herself as more irritable since their onset. She and her family were mystified by what they saw as the major and apparently unaccountable changes in her. Other people with specific health problems report feeling that others cannot under stand their reaction even if they understand it themselves, for example, "YOU CAN'T EXPECT A MAN

TO UNDERSTAND HOW YOU FEEL AFTER HAVING A HYSTERECTOMY."

Many of the images of uncertainty which have been most vivid have come from people who have recently had strokes and are dealing with the resulting paralyses. Cerebro-vascular accidents occur without warning: "IT CAME OUT OF THE BLUE." People do not necessarily feel ill or tired beforehand: "I WOULD NEVER HAVE THOUGHT ANYTHING LIKE THIS WAS GOING TO HAPPEN TO ME." Its effects can be catastrophic, "SUDDENLY I COULDN'T MOVE", and lasting, "I'M NOT USED TO JUST LYING IN BED." Their future begins to look unpredictable: "I DON'T KNOW HOW I'M GOING TO COPE." Also, the reaction of their family and friends is likely to be unpredictable, confusing and poorly informed: "I DON'T KNOW HOW MY WIFE WILL FEEL WITH ME LIKE THIS", "THINGS ARE IN CHAOS AT HOME" and "THEY DON'T REALLY KNOW MUCH ABOUT STROKES." Having a stroke leads to much uncertainty.

The Implications of Images of Uncertainty

We have seen how the ill people who have contributed to this research had constructed images of uncertainty when they were initially informed about their problem. A literature search has shown that other researchers have reported this finding, for illnesses as different as diabetes (Engelmann, 1976; Mason, 1985), heart conditions (Farber, 1978) and cancer (Rosenbaum, 1975; Bard and Sutherland, 1977; Wortman and Dunkel-Schetter, 1979). They have found, too, evidence for such images in relation to the illness or injury itself, its treatment, their future and the reactions of others (Jessop and Stein, 1985). Images of these kinds have been described, and the comments of people with strokes, especially have provided appropriate examples.

Consider, also, the uncertainty of people who have found themselves to test positive for the HIV antibody (Cassens, 1985), with the strong possibility that they will develop AIDS. They are often initially shocked (Grant and Anns, 1988), with an associated numbness and confusion (Miller, 1987). These images of uncertainty are sometimes associated with loss of hope (Miller and Brown, 1988). These people are concerned with the as yet not fully known implications of AIDS (Dilley et al., 1985; Faulstich, 1987).

Researchers have, however, not merely identified images of uncertainty. They have gone on to look at the implications these images have for anyone trying to deal with illness-related events. They have explored how these images have developed from people's experiences of illness, and the extent to which they determine our resistance to illness and our recovery from it. Their findings are now considered. There is, for example, general agreement among them that images of uncertainty are constructed by people who are ill when they cannot find meaning in what is happening to them (Mechanic, 1974; Janis and Rodin, 1979; Yalom, 1980). It is younger people who are ill as well as those who have less education, who have less direct and vicarious experience to draw on and so construct more of these images (Viney and Westbrook, 1982a).

People need to find meaning in the symptoms of their illness (Cowie, 1976), and to make them more predictable (Forsyth, Delaney and Gresham, 1984). They also need to reformulate the meanings their affected body part has for them and to deal with changes in their body image (Lipowski, 1967). They need to find meaning in their new life style (Mechanic, 1977). Without clarifying these meanings for themselves, they cannot cope with the resulting stress (Silver and Wortman, 1980). Without remodelling old images and building new ones people cannot be ready to make the decisions about their own health care which it is their right to make. Ill people have all these tasks to accomplish; but they are not easy. There are aspects of their illness and its treatment which can make it difficult for anyone to construct useful images and develop meaningful interpretations.

Ill people and physicians alike often find that their expectations of each other are not born out (Reichman, 1981). People with life threatening and physically debilitating diseases, like cancer, can find their time perspectives for both short and long time spans considerably altered (Straus, 1975; Mages and Mendelsohn, 1979). Isolation in an intensive care unit, for example after a heart attack, can have this effect too (Hackett, Cassem and Wishnie, 1968; Johnson and Sarason, 1978), as can haemodialysis for those with kidney problems (Adams, 1970). As to the longer view, illness has been demonstrated to make future planning difficult (Hamburg, 1974; Moos and Tsu, 1977). Hospitalization has also been shown to make it difficult for ill and injured people to construct useful images. This can be because of a lack of relatively simple, concrete bits of information about hospital routines and hierarchies (Volicer, 1978). It can also be a more fundamental loss of meaning: a loss of identity and continuity brought about by the depersonalization of those same hospital routines and hierarchies (Cassell, 1976).

There is evidence that uncertainty-laden images may play a role in reducing peoples' resistance to illness (Le Shan, 1977). Several decades of research have suggested that people who experience more major changes in their lives are more prone to illness and injury than those who have experienced fewer changes (Cleghorn and Streiner, 1979; Gunderson and Rahe, 1974; Rahe and Arthur, 1978). These changes are transitions, or sometimes crises, during which peoples' cognitive grip on their lives is loosened and many images of uncertainty are constructed (Viney, 1980). They can be changes which are made voluntarily (such as marriage or a change of job) or involuntarily (such as the death of a loved one or the loss of one's job). It seems that uncertainty may make people more vulnerable to illness (Hinkle, 1974), although the form of the relationship is not yet clear (Hurst, Jenkins and Rose, 1976). It may be that the images which preclude uncertainty - coherence, continuity and confidence - give people insulation against viruses, infections, neoplasms and accidents (Antonovsky, 1979).

Be that as it may, once people become ill or involved in accidents, their uncertainty-laden images can affect their recovery.

Evidence of this is available from a number of sources. People do not recover so well from surgery if they are uncertain (Cohen and Lazarus, 1973). People hospitalized with severe burns have been shown to recover more slowly if they are passive and poorly informed about their physical state and their future (Andreasen, Noyes and Hartford, 1972). People with cancer have been found not to adjust so well to the problems it brings, if they passively accept it and do not actively seek information about it (Worden and Sobel, 1978). Of course these descriptions of associations do not tell us whether people who are more uncertain adjust poorly or whether people who adjust poorly are more uncertain. Perhaps both statements are true. That this relationship may be causal has been suggested by a study of people after heart attacks. When they were supplied with information about their condition and progress they proved likely to recover more quickly, need fewer tranquilisers and sedatives and experience better quality of life, than those who were not (Doehrman, 1977). Images of uncertainty, it seems, interfere with recovery from illness and injury.

Coping with Images of Uncertainty

In this first chapter of Section 2 I examined some examples of negative images of uncertainty. They have been developed by people to cope with having the news broken to them about their illness, with the illness itself and with its treatment. They are also stimulated when people try to deal with their future and the reactions to them of their family and friends. Other researchers have confirmed that uncertainty is often a reaction to illness and injury and have gone some way to explore why this is so. They have also linked uncertainty images with poor resistance to illness as well as poor recovery from it. It now remains to make some suggestions about how images of uncertainty may be broken down. For this, ill and injured people need the help of family, friends, and health care professionals. Whoever works with them, providing they come to understand the images which the ill person uses to interpret his or her world, can provide a form of crisis counselling. This can be especially fruitful before surgery. A dialogue of this kind is provided. Finally, the role of the ill or injured person as their own decision-maker is emphasized.

For anybody working with ill or injured people, whether to reduce their uncertainty or for some other purpose, the first thing to recognize is that everyone - counsellor and counselled - can only interpret events by using the images available to them (Kelly, 1955). This means, for example, that there was no point in trying to help that elderly man who had an image of "acceptance" to "cope." This new and alien image of "coping" was too far from his particular frame of reference to make sense to him (Landfield, 1965). Of course as the counsellor and counselled work together, they come to share some of the meanings of their respective images (Viney, 1981a). Their chief focus, however, is on the images of those who are counselled (Neimeyer, R.A., 1987). Their aim is to widen the range of choices available to them (Keen, 1977; Fransella, 1985). These statements hold whether the counsellor is a health care professional, or not professionally trained but a concerned family member or friend.

People who are ill, on the other hand, should recognize that images of uncertainty are likely to be common for them during their time of crisis, that is, during the early stages of their illness (Pasewark and Albers, 1972; Golan, 1978). A counsellor can use a counselling process like the one described above to help them deal with their uncertainty. One way to do this is to focus the attention of ill people who are plagued by uncertainty on the more structured and therefore meaningful aspects of their lives, that is, those parts which they do understand and control. They can help them to use their already existing images to differentiate among aspects of the events which lead to uncertainty. They can also aid them in anticipating stressors that they will have to deal with in the future, whether these stressors involve beginning a new and frightening treatment programme or coming to the end of one which had promised much but achieved little (Holland et al., 1977). All of this must be done with an eye to the speed at which the ill people can do this psychological work. People cannot generate images, test them, and then elaborate or refashion them very quickly (Kelly, 1955). The timing of the counsellor is very important.

A useful set of techniques by which counsellors can help people who have many images of uncertainty about the outcomes of their illness have been developed by psychotherapists dealing with people with cancer (Moorey and Greer, 1987). They advocate facing fears about disabling and distressing symptoms and keeping better informed about likely illness outcomes (Rainey, 1985). They recommend having people identify and test self-defeating automatic thoughts about the progress of their illness and planning enjoyable activities both for the pleasure of them and as a distraction (Beck et al., 1979). They also encourage people dealing with illness to value the uncertain images they have about it. This process involves valueing them as proof that they personally are flexible and reality-oriented rather than rigid and reality-distorting, as people who use denial to cope with illness can be.

This is not to say that ill people cannot come to terms themselves with their own uncertainty. Some of their uncertainty is likely to reside in confusion about who they now are, what they want from their new life, the directions in which they are heading and even about how they feel about all this. One way of clarifying this inner uncertainty is to pay attention to the series of images we all experience periodically without choosing to become aware of them: our dreams. Selecting dreams which are immediately recorded and involve much emotion and several concrete and vivid images has been recommended for this purpose (Gendlin, 1985; Gottschalk, 1985; Mahrer, 1971). It is believed that dreams represent parts of us or our potentials which we have not yet accepted or achieved, and that dreams are a way of becoming aware of those potentials (Mahrer, 1979; 1983). Interpretation of these potentials, especially in the light of current significant illness-related events is the goal. The feedback available from acting on these dream interpretations provides valuable information about the extent to which those uncertainty-arousing images have been internally interpreted. It may be, too, that identification of some potentials in this way not only reduced uncertainty but identifies the blocks to meaningful self-expression which have contributed to people's vulnerability to disease (Le Shan, 1977).

A brief account of a dialogue between a man waiting in hospital for surgery for his haemorroids and an experienced nurse, follows. Surgery can have different meaning for different people (Chapman and Cox, 1977). In this account, her focus is on the more structured aspects of his life, his use of his own images built on his own experiences and his successful attempts at differentiation, are apparent.

Nurse: "Good morning, Mr. W. I hear that you are having your haemorroids operated on today; and I called to see if there is anything you might want to talk about before the operation."

George W.: "No., nothing much. (Pause). I've taken the time to get it done at last. The doctor says I've let it go too long."

Nurse: "Haemorroids are pretty painful things to leave too long, aren't they?"

George W.: "You can say that again! Three years of burning and aching..."

Nurse: "I'm wondering why you waited."

George W.: "Oh well, I didn't know what it would be like. Besides, I've got the business to run."

Nurse: "How are you managing to run that while you're in here?"

George W.: "I know I've got a good partner. And my wife is in the office. And the men in the field are good too. No worries there."

Nurse: "It sounds as if you've got that well organized. Have you been able to ask your doctor all you wanted to about the operation?"

George W.: "Oh yes. I suppose operations these days are better. I've only been in hospital once before, when I was 14, and I had my tonsils out. I remember the anaesthetic. They put a thing over my face and I faught like a demon. I thought I was going to choke to death. And vomit after! For hours!"

Nurse: "Those were the bad old days! Now, you'll find it very different." (An account of her experience of modern anaesthetics followed).

George W.: "You wouldn't kid me. Have you actually had it yourself?"

Nurse: "Yes, I've had it several times."

George W.: "What about after - the vomiting?"

Nurse: "People don't usually vomit after this anaesthetic, but you can ask your anaesthetist about it when he comes to see you in an hour or so."

George W.: "He'll probably think I'm chicken."

Nurse: "I'm sure he'll be very pleased that you are sensible enough to ask about what is going to be done to you."

George W.: "Fair enough! It is me , who's getting it done, not him."

There is evidence that preparation for surgery helps people cope better with it psychologically and recover more quickly from it physically (Janis, 1955; Schmitt and Woolridge, 1973; Vernon and Bigelow, 1974). It can also aid people dealing with more minor but nonetheless distressing operations such as swallowing tubes for diagnostic procedures (Johnson and Leventhal, 1974). It may be that it is not only images of uncertainty that are modified by such preparation but anxiety-laden images as well (Janis and Rodin, 1979). I will examine such work in Chapter 4. Not everyone is helped by this kind of preparation. Some people who are ill and injured, like some people facing other kinds of threat, prefer not to be aware of them. Avoiders and deniers put such threats out of their minds, sometimes in the teeth of a lot of evidence (Hackett, Cassem and Wishnie, 1968; Croog, Shapiro and Levine, 1971; Polivy, 1977; Sanders and Kardinal, 1977). Such people, who persist in using images of their illness which diverge far from the information available to them, do not make good use of pre-operative preparation (Andrew, 1970).

To conclude this chapter I would like to return to some of the last words of George W.: "It is me who's getting it done." While people who are ill or injured remain responsibly aware, it is their right to make decisions about their own treatment. This can be difficult; because decisions like that of George, to have his operation, can have unpleasant consequences. Avoiders and deniers do not stay with such difficult decisions to the extent that people do who gather whatever relevant information they can. A "balance sheet" can be set out to weigh up the pros and cons or the gains and risks of any procedure. This is one way in which people who are ill can make and maintain such decisions (Janis and Mann, 1977). Decisions are best made by people with few uncertainty-laden images.

CHAPTER 4

ANXIETY-LADEN IMAGES

"I'll be scared until this operation is over".

(Betty, D., appendectomy)

Anxiety-laden images contain fears, threats and worries and also some very unpleasant feelings. Let me examine one such image constructed by someone who was seriously ill, in some detail. "I'VE BEEN UNDER A LOT OF STRESS LATELY." The man who said this had recently had a heart attack; and this was one image he was trying out to see if it accounted for that attack. Moreover, he was wondering whether, if he experienced such stress in the future, he would have another attack. He was also talking of pressures he felt to be on him, of demands made of him by business associates and friends but also by himself. And he was reporting signs of tension in his body which he had been experiencing: stiff muscles, occasional headaches and tiredness. He was also saying that he had known what it was like not to experience stress. An image expressed in just a single sentence can lead to a complex set of implications.

That anxiety-laden image was being used by the man who constructed it to account for what had happened to him. People trying to plan a future which hasn't happened yet also use these images. When people who are ill do this, their future is often bleak. Their images often focus, then, on specific fears. They may fear damage to their bodies from a procedure being carried out to help them. For example, "I'M SCARED OF THIS OPERATION" is a statement that might be made by most people facing surgery. While death is a relatively unlikely outcome of surgery, there are plenty of other unpleasant consequences to fear. There is being temporarily unaware of what happens, the discomfort of awakening, pain at the site of the operation and fear about the severity of the problem which may have been revealed, to name a few. Together with these concerns, come the sweaty palms or queasiness which each of us recognizes as our unique bodily signs of anxiety.

I have said that death is a relatively unusual outcome for many severely ill or injured people, and they respond according to the images they have of it. I am reminded of a lady who was successfully fighting cancer. She had faced death and drawn back from it. Reflecting on this experience, she said: "I THOUGHT I WAS GOING TO DIE, SO I DIDN'T BUY ANYTHING NEW." Since many people would go on a spending spree under such circumstances, I was intrigued by this image and asked her to explain it to me. She replied that she and her husband had needed a new bed for some time; but that, when she realized how ill she was, she had decided not to buy one. As she said: "IT SEEMED SO SILLY WHEN I DIDN'T HAVE LONG. I KEPT THINKING THAT HE WOULDN'T WANT TO TAKE A NEW WIFE TO BED IN OUR OLD BED, SO HE COULD HAVE A NEW ONE WHEN HE NEEDED IT."

A range of anxiety-laden images will now be described. Some of them involve vague, general anxiety, and also the direct denial of that anxiety. Others, like those already examined, deal with fears of body damage from both the actual illness or injury and its treatment, and with fears of death. Images of death constructed by seriously ill people seem to fall into two categories: the recognition of the increased risk of death and realistic preparation for it. They are stimulated by having to cope with the deaths of others. How all of these images are used, by cancer patients for example, will also be discussed.

Some Anxiety-Laden Images of Illness

General anxiety occurs in images relating to many aspects of illness. Some people associate it with their reactions to hospital life. "IT PROVES THAT YOU HAVE GOT NERVES." Others are concerned about how long their hospitalization is going to keep them away from their normal activities: "I'M ONLY WORRIED ABOUT HOW LONG I'M GOING TO BE OFF MY FEET." Then there are those who recognize that illness is making them more anxious: "DIABETICS TEND TO MAKE MOUNTAINS OUT OF MOLEHILLS" and "BEING ILL, IT'S DOUBLE THE WEIGHT AND DOUBLE THE PRESSURE." Of course pain is a common focus of anxiety-laden images: "I GO UP THE WALL WITH THE PAIN SOMETIMES." So, for the disabled, is keeping oneself mobile: "KEEPING THE WHEELCHAIR GOING IS ANOTHER PROBLEM I'VE GOT." And families can make their contribution too: "I CAN SEE MYSELF GETTING UPSET ABOUT THINGS AT HOME. IT DOESN'T DO ME MUCH GOOD."

Some people, as I mentioned in Chapter 3, prefer to avoid or deny their more disturbing feelings such as anxiety. Some people, however, remain dimly aware of such feelings but build images of themselves in which, what they see as weakness is denied. "BEING IN HOSPITAL DOES NOT WORRY ME A BIT." "I'VE NEVER HAD ANY TROUBLE WITH THE DIABETES." At other times they go further and provide images with determinedly positive feelings to mask the more negative ones, for example, "YOU JUST KEEP YOUR OLD CHIN UP." In both cases, anxiety is likely to be present. This tendency to deny disruptive emotions is greater earlier rather than later in the course of the illness. Many images involving fears of body damage have been presented to us. Some of them have been related to the catastrophic effects of illness. "I WAS IN HERE HAEMORRAGING IN MARCH AND MAY" (genito-urinary problems). "WHEN I HAD THE STROKE IT LEFT ME ALL OF A HEAP" (cerebro-vascular accident). "I GET A LOT OF BLADDER PROBLEMS" (quadraplegia). "HAVING ANOTHER HEART ATTACK DID SO MUCH DAMAGE TO IT" (myocardial infarction). "THIS LEG IS TOO FAR GONE FOR ME TO WALK ON" (diseased tibia). "IT'S A HORRIBLE THING I'M FACED WITH" (cancer). Accidents, too, take their toll: "I INJURED MY BACK AT WORK" and "TWO WEEKS AGO I HAD AN ACCIDENT ON MY MOTORBIKE."

The reader may expect anxiety-laden images from people suffering such catastrophes. You may be less likely to expect them to be experiencing such fear of the treatments prescribed for them. Yet such is the case. Operations, especially, are approached with fear. Sometimes this fear comes from ignorance. "THEY ARE GOING TO BREAK THE BONES IN MY KNEES", as one elderly and deaf lady confided. More often it is included in images which have been tested against physical reality and found to be reasonably accurate. "I'M JUST UNLUCKY WITH THE OPERATIONS - I'VE HAD SO MANY OF THEM." "I'LL BE SCARED UNTIL THIS OPERATION IS OVER." "IF HE WAS TO OPERATE ON THE ULCER ITSELF, I COULD WIND UP AN

INVALID." In all of these examples, body damage is the focus of the image. Images of death have also been quite common among our informants. Many of them are constructed in order to cope with the recognized nearness of it. Sometimes it is in the form of a long range warning: "THE DOCTOR SAID TO ME ABOUT MY EATING SWEETS AND THINGS WITH DIABETES, 'YOU'RE TAKING YOUR LIFE IN YOUR HANDS'". More often it is a closer call like this one of heart failure on the operating table, "IT WAS TOO CLOSE". Another dimly recognized the threat: "THE PRIEST WAS ANNOINTING ME AND THAT, AS IF I WERE ALMOST DEAD." At other times it is possible to construct more complex images, such as "I FELT AS THOUGH MY LIFE WERE OVER" and "I THOUGHT TO MYSELF, YOU'RE NEVER GOING TO SEE THE CHILDREN GROW UP."

Faced with imminent death, some people construct images which enable them to prepare realistically for it. "I'M READY TO GO ANY TIME NOW." "I'VE MADE MY WILL OUT." One father of a large family was very pleased to hear that his third son had just succeeded in getting his drivers' license: "EVEN IF I DIE NOW, THE FAMILY WILL BE ABLE TO MANAGE." Both types of images of death, recognition and preparation images, are of course stimulated by the deaths of others. Two such images make this clear. "I'VE SEEN A LOT OF MY GAY FRIENDS DYING BEFORE ME FROM AIDS, AND THAT BRINGS THE NEARNESS OF DEATH HOME TO ME." "HAVING LOST A HUSBAND WITH CANCER, IT'S PRETTY SCARY TO HAVE IT YOURSELF."

Cancer seems to stimulate anxiety-laden images. Cancer

sufferers have described to us images of all of the kinds that have been examined. General anxiety dominates their view of the world: "I LET EVERYTHING WORRY ME NOW." They fear body damage from the cancer, "THERE ISN'T ONE PART OF MY BODY IT HASN'T AFFECTED"; and they fear it from the treatments to which they are exposed, "I CAN'T LET MY SKIN BE IN THE SUN AFTER THAT DRUG THERAPY." They are well aware of the risk of death: "AFTER THAT SURGERY, I WAS LUCKY TO BE ALIVE." Many of them can also see the gains as well as the losses of imminent death: "WHEN DEATH IS JUST IN FRONT OF YOU, YOU ARE AFRAID BUT YOU DO GET OUT AND DO MORE." Cancer sufferers, too, need to build images when confronted by death by cancer in others: "I'VE GOT THE BIG C. BIG JOHN WAYNE WAS GOING TO BEAT IT... BUT IT GOT HIM IN THE END... I WONDER HOW I'LL GO..."

The Implications of Anxiety-Laden Images

A variety of anxiety-laden images has been described. They have included statements representing images of general anxiety, as well as images which deny such anxiety. They have also included images of body damage from the actual illness or accident and from their treatment. Some images of death have been dealt with, too, focussing on the recognition of the risk of death and realistic preparation for it. How these images can come to be important, for example for cancer sufferers, has also been examined. It is now appropriate to turn to the findings of other researchers concerning these images: how they are generated by illness and some of its treatments, how they affect recovery from illness and how they can make people more vulnerable to illness.

Anxiety-laden images have been found to be associated with illness (Cassell, 1976; Moos and Tsu, 1977; Early and Redfearing, 1979; Derogatis, 1986). In fact they have been found to be more commonly used by people dealing with a variety of illnesses (Viney, 1980; Viney and Westbrook, 1982c; Westbrook and Viney, 1981; 1982). Some of these are AIDS (Grant and Anns, 1988; Holland and Tross, 1985; Namir, et al., 1987; Viney et al., 1987), diabetes (Engelmann, 1976; Viney and Westbrook, 1986), cancer (Bard and Sutherland, 1977; Gottschalk and Hoigaard, 1986; Greer, 1985; Lewis and Bloom, 1978-79; Worden & Weisman, 1984; Wortman and Dunkel-Schetter, 1979) and heart disease (Byrne and Whyte, 1978; Dorossiev, Paskova and Zachariev, 1976; Hlatky et al., 1986; Stocksmeier, 1976). People with heart problems have received considerable attention. They have been found to have many anxiety-dominated images immediately after a heart attack. The number of their images falls during hospitalization but rises again on discharge (Dellipiani et al ., 1976). This high level of anxiety has been known to continue for months for people with heart conditions (Rodda, Miller and Bruhn, 1976; Wiklund et al., 1984).

Anxiety-laden images are also stimulated by some of the treatments provided for people who are ill. Cardiac care units are an example of this effect (Hackett, Cassem and Wishnie, 1968), together with haemodialysis for people with kidney failure (Abram, 1970), radiotherapy after mastectomy for women (Holland et al ., 1979) and bone marrow transplants for people with leukaemia (Wellisch, Fawzy and Yager, 1978). Hospitalization, too, seems to give rise to higher levels of anxiety. This occurs regardless of the type of illness or injury people are dealing with; but it seems to vary according to hospital type. Larger hospitals and teaching hospitals seem to generate more anxiety than smaller, country hospitals (Lucente and Fleck, 1972).

Images involving fears of body damage are important contributors to ill people's level of general anxiety. This seems to be the case for people with cancer (Mages and Mendelsohn, 1979), but also for those with other kinds of chronic disease (Abram, 1972; Viney, 1980; 1984). In another study, we asked people with chronic disease about the extent to which they saw themselves as handicapped. Four areas of handicap were examined: mobility, self-care, leisure and relationships. People who saw themselves as severely handicapped, especially in their mobility, were found to use a lot of images involving fear of body damage (Viney and Westbrook, 1982b). There is no equivalent information about how some treatments stimulate such fears. This has not yet become an area of investigation. The images of the ill and injured people who have spoken with us while participating in this research programme, however, have indicated how real these fears have been for them.

Images involving fears of death are important contributors to the general level of anxiety of ill people (Cohen and Lazarus, 1979; Mages and Mendelsohn, 1979; Viney, 1980; 1984; 1986-87; Thurer, Levine and Thurer, 1980-81). There can also be vivid images of feared death constructed by people who are not ill (Glaser and Strauss, 1968). In fact, young and middle-aged people have been reported to fear death more in this culture than elderly people for whom it is likely to be closer (Weisman and Kastenbaum, 1968). Perhaps this is because we have, in our society, what amounts to a cultural denial of death (Weisman, 1972; van den Berg, 1980). It is not surprising that people facing death may, at least for a time, deny their anxiety about it (Katz et al., 1970). Ways of coping with death have been developed for people who are having difficulty in doing so (Kubler-Ross, 1969). Fears of death, however, are still common among people with chronic illness (Viney, 1980), especially in those who have severe communication difficulties brought about by disabilities of speech, hearing and sight (Viney and Westbrook, 1982b). For all of us it is as important to construct some meaningful image of death as it is of life (Lofland, 1978; Rowe, 1981).

While the dying person has multiple losses to deal with (Benoiel, 1985), most illness leads to loss of some kind (Keltikangas-Jlarvinen, 1986). This is as true of ulcerative colitis (Lloyd and Laurence, 1985), as it is of foetal malformation for pregnant women (Kelly, 1986). When such losses occur, peoples' images of illness and of other events in their lives become inflexible and only poorly related to reality (Viney, 1985b). A long period of grieving for the loss is necessary before they cope effectively again (Viney, Benjamin and Preston, in pressc). Grieving is resolved either through changing one's images or through changing events to fit with one's images (Woodfield and Viney, 1985). When the images are illness-related, however, this may be difficult to do.

The information available about the effects of anxiety-laden images on people's rehabilitation and recovery will surprise some readers. Because anxiety is unpleasant, we tend to think of its effects as bad rather than good. In fact, in dealing with the stresses of illness and injury, just as with other kinds of stress (Levitt,1967), too much or too little anxiety can make for difficulties. A moderate amount of manageable anxiety can be helpful. People with some anxiety-laden images have been found to recover from surgery more quickly than those with fewer images (Johnson and Carpenter, 1980). People with some anxiety-laden images have survived cancer longer than those with fewer such images (Katz et al., 1970; Derogatis and Abeloff, 1979). A similar effect has been observed for people with heart conditions (Blumenthal et al., 1979). Indeed, for a range of chronic illnesses the early construction of anxiety-laden images has been associated with good rehabilitation later (Viney and Westbrook, 1982c). The only work I know of which disputes these claims has been with people with heart problems who, if they had many images of anxiety, tended to have a more complicated recovery in hospital than those who did not (Pancheri et al., 1978); but their anxiety levels may have been very high.

The weight of this evidence suggests that to be aware of some mild anxiety-laden images during illness may be helpful. The available evidence about stress and people's vulnerability to illness leads us to a different conclusion about the effects. Stress has been associated with increased illness generally (Canter, Imboden and Cluff, 1966), and with the onset of specific diseases. People using many anxiety-laden images seem to be more open to infection (Meyer and

Haggerty, 1962), more liable to develop gastro-intestinal problems such as ulcers (Kasanen and Forsstrom, 1966), and more likely to suffer from hypertension (Shapiro, 1978) and heart disease (Reeder, 1973; Schar, Reeder and Dirkens, 1973). Heart disease, which has been examined in more detail than other diseases, may be stimulated by the way people manage their anxiety (Dembroski et al., 1978; Friedman and Rosenman, 1974; Haynes et al., 1978; Siegrist and Halhuber, 1981). If they ignore and deny it (Radley and Green, 1985), they may experience no anxiety-laden images; but their bodies will continue to react as if they are anxious. It may be this constant state of readiness to deal with stress without a controlling awareness of it which imposes too much strain on the cardiovascular system.

Coping with Anxiety-Laden Images

Many examples of anxiety-laden images have been described in this chapter. They have included images which are dominated by general anxiety, stimulated both by illness and the treatment prescribed for it. They have also included more specific anxieties, that is, fears of body damage, of death and of other losses. It has been noted, too, that some people, at least for a time, seem to avoid or deny their anxiety so as to produce images which can be very limited as guides to the real world. There is evidence from studies, other than this one, that illness and injury stimulate anxiety-laden images, including that relating to body damage and death. There is less information available about people's fears of treatment procedures. The effects of anxiety-laden images on people's rehabilitation and recovery seem, in the main, to be good.

Expression of anxiety about illness, then, is appropriate. However, the experience of anxiety seems to be linked in a causative way with the development of various types of illness. It is therefore important to know how to manage anxiety (Forester, Kornfeld and Fleiss, 1982; Greer and Moorey, 1987; Viney, Benjamin and Preston in press d; Viney et al., 1985a; b). However, suggestions dealing with denial and avoidance of anxiety-laden images in others are made before turning to the control of anxiety at facilitating levels. How to help people deal with imminent death is also considered. Finally, another dialogue is presented in which the causative role of anxiety-laden images in the onset of illness can be seen.

Denial can be more comfortable for people coping with the threat of severe illness or even its treatment, so long as no active dealing with the source of the threat can be effective. If people can do something to avert the threat, denial and avoidance of it take that opportunity away from them. The split which exists between image and reality becomes too wide. They can no longer cope realistically; and more anxiety arises from this failure. The way to help others out of such a vicious circle is to help them focus on their strengths. Often when people are able to remember how effectively they coped with other situations, it gives them the strength to cope with their current one, their illness. Sometimes they find, too, that the same coping strategies they used before will work for them now (Rowe, 1987). For example, "WHEN I WAS GOING THROUGH THAT BAD PATCH WITH MY FAMILY, I JUST HUNG ON UNTIL IT BLEW OVER. MAY BE I CAN DO THAT AGAIN."

[or] "WHEN MY HUSBAND LEFT ME, I WAS BESIDE MYSELF AT FIRST. BUT I KEPT BUSY. IF I KEEP BUSY NOW....."

There is another form of avoidance or denial people use, in which it is not the anxiety they do not acknowledge, but the part of their body which is causing them discomfort and disability. For example, a man with a diseased tibia said: "I'd rather go to the bathroom than have a bed pan; but the leg won't let me." The offending leg was not being recognized by him as his own leg, connected to his body, but as an alien object over which he had no control. This psychological lack of body integration seems unlikely to promote healing. Anyone working with ill or injured people in a counselling role should take care to integrate such disowned parts in his or her statements. To return to the example, the counsellor might say: "Is that because your leg is painful?" Drawing a picture of themselves to include the body part can also lead to better integration, since people, while drawing, often begin to explore their images of that part, its treatment and its chances of recovery.

The reactions of these people to their illness or injury have involved relatively little anxiety. Many people facing such sources of stress, in contrast, tend to be overwhelmed by their anxiety-laden images. Such images can interfere, for example, with their role as decision-maker, which was mentioned in Chapter 3, as well as with their physical recovery (Viney et al., 1985c). However, understanding likely reactions to stress, acquiring new coping skills and applying them to the stresses of illness can provide a kind of innoculation against stress. This approach has proved effective with a variety of stresses, including one which is very salient for some ill people - pain (Melzak, 1980; Turk and Genest, 1979; Keefe and Dolan, 1986). These coping skills can include strategies as different as understanding how anxiety works and planning enjoyable distractions. In order to help people adhere to some of the difficult decisions they must make another technique has been devised. People are asked to think of as many positive but realistic consequences of, say, surgery, as they can, for example, a rest in hospital and feeling better after it. When their anxiety-laden images flood into awareness, they are asked to keep these consequences in mind (Langner, Janis and Wolfer, 1975). This technique can work well. What these two stress innoculation techniques have in common is that they can help people to modify their anxiety-laden images of illness (Girodo, 1977).

But to return to the anxiety centred on death, how can people be helped to deal with it? It is important to remember that, for people facing death, anxiety is only one of many emotions they may experience (Kubler Ross, 1969) as they try to come to terms with the personal meanings it has for them. It may mean a cutting off from loved ones or a release from pain and discomfort. It may mean an end to life or the beginning of a new one (Rowe, 1981). Often there is little time in which to aid people in clarifying these images. The goal of thanatological counselling, then, is to help people construct a set of images of death which permits them to be comfortable with themselves and what they believe is to come (Feigenberg and Schneidman, 1979). This can involve maintaining some stability in their world, aiding them in tying off any loose ends in their life and generally making sure that things go as well as possible. The accepting and honest person who offers these services to people who are dying is much valued by them, whether he or she be relative, friend or professional health care giver. The same services are also needed by those who are left (Viney, in pressc).

This chapter ends with an example of how anxiety-laden images can generate physical symptoms and how changing some of these images can relieve such symptoms. Georgia G. had had severe pains in her neck and head for three years. Extensive medical tests showed no signs of physical damage; but she was leading the restricted life of an invalid. Although no-one questioned that this young woman was experiencing pain, Georgia was worried that people might think she was malingering. Her illness-related images are apparent in what she says.

Georgia: "Someone said it was probably my nerves."

Counsellor: "What do you think she meant by that?"

Georgia: "That I imagine the pain because I'm a nervous person."

Counsellor: "Did you know that anxiety and tension cause real, physical pain, especially where you're getting it - in your neck and head?"

Georgia: "The pain is real all right - but if it is only nerves...."

Counsellor: "OK. If you're nervous, you tighten up, don't you? You're pretty upset right now; so feel the muscles in your neck, here, with your fingers. Are they tight?"

Georgia: "I don't know. Don't they have to be to hold my head up?"

Counsellor: "Will you try something that will show whether they are tight or not?"

The differential muscle relaxation technique was then used, followed by relaxation therapy (Rimm and Masters, 1978). Georgia learned not only how to detect when her neck muscles were unnecessarily tense, but also how to relax them at will. She achieved this with professional help; but much of the work she did herself at home using tape-recorded instructions. She also gave up many of the images which she had applied to her pain. Six months later she was playing tennis regularly and helping her husband redecorate their house. She had had no return of the pain.

The muscle relaxation technique can be useful for ill people who are dealing with distressing emotions such as anxiety. It involves learning to relax specific muscle groups at will, until a general relaxation has been achieved. It is not easy for some people to learn because they need help in recognizing when their muscles are tensed and when relaxed. Georgia needed little of this help. While this technique can lead to a cessation of pain as it did in Georgia's case, it seems to work best in combination with other techniques. With migraine headaches, for example, it has been found to provide some relief when used together with monitoring of the occurrence of headaches and of the stressors which precede them. The most effective treatment, however, was one which also encouraged the migraine sufferers to become aware of and break down some of their own anxiety-laden images (Mitchell and White, 1977). Recognizing one's own anxiety-laden images is very important for ill people, and family as well as health care professionals can help them do this if they take the time to listen to them in an accepting way.

CHAPTER 5

ANGER-LADEN IMAGES

"I hate being in hospital!"

(Phil. C., multiple fractures)

Anger can range in its expression from aggression to hostility. It can stimulate a variety of actions from assertive exploration of one's world to determined and sometimes explosive attempts to maintain the images one is using at all costs. It may take the form of mild irritation which encourages those who experience it to deal promptly with some annoyingly discrepant aspects of their lives (Kelly, 1955). It may also take the form of wild outbursts against the people and events of one's world. The first kind of anger provides an effective antidote to the images of helplessness that beset many ill and injured people. (I will explore helplessness images more fully in Chapter 6). The second kind of anger is less controlled. Because it is explosive, its expression needs careful handling. Sometimes this hostility, lacking any other outlet, finds its expression in physical illness, such as a cancerous growth.

Some anger-laden images of illness will now be examined in detail. For example, "I'M FED UP WITH BEING SICK ALL THE TIME" is a statement which has been made to us frequently by people suffering from chronic illness. It represents an image which implies exasperation with illness, especially with the way it is always present and permeates every aspect of life. There is a note of despair, too, in that phrase "all the time". There seems never to be any respite. Finally, the metaphor used to express the anger is one which adds much to the meaning of the statement. "I am fed up" suggests an unpleasant, stuffed and almost choking feeling like that which follows over-eating. The next step might well be to vomit; except that illness cannot be vomitted up. This image of endurance nearing breaking point is a strong one.

"THERE'S NOTHING TO DO IN HOSPITAL" is an image which represents how people see, not their illness, but the results of their illness. It has some elements in common with the earlier image; for example, the despair in the exaggerated phrasing of "There is nothing..." which echoes that of "...all the time". There is anger common to both images. In this example, too, the anger stems from frustration that the speaker cannot do something - anything - while she is in hospital. For her, this may be a minor irritation. If continued, this enforced inaction could lead to major outbursts of hostility. Implicit in her statement, too, are elements of blame. "Why am I not kept entertained?" "Why do the staff make me lie here like this for so long?" "My needs to be active and feel useful - are not being met in this place".

These two images convey the second kind of anger which has been described here, hostility. The third image to be described is of the first kind. "I'M LOOKING FORWARD TO BEING FIT ENOUGH TO FIGHT ANOTHER DAY" conjures up an image of a healthy person enjoying the challenges the world presents. These challenges may involve damsels in distress waiting for their knight in shining armour or they may involve the Red Baron waiting for the Snoopy in us all. The central theme is one of a challenge to be met with bravery and skill. If to be well is to be fit to fight such battles, then to be ill is to feel overwhelmed by illness, to lack the bravery and skill needed to deal with it and what it brings. In its more positive form, however, this image represents a frame of reference which encourages active exploration of one's world.

The rest of this chapter deals, like those before it, with some of the images which have been presented to us by people who are ill. Some of these anger-laden images have to do with other people - with friends and relatives, and with health care staff. More often they focus on the illness or injury which is the major source of frustration, the treatments prescribed for them and some of their other effects. Anger is not always expressed directly. People's ways of denying the existence of angry feelings in themselves are also explored. The customary survey of the relevant literature is also included here. The information available about what aspects of illness are associated with anger is considered, as is that suggesting that anger may cause illness. The role of anger, and its expression, during the course of an illness is also evaluated. Finally, I make some suggestions about how to cope with anger. A case study illustrates how assertion-promoting anger can be used to good effect. Open expression of anger is encouraged, together with exploration of the emotions and bodily sensation associated with anger-laden images. Meditation is described as a useful tool for coping with self-defeating anger. Avoidance of unnecessary frustration is recommended.

Some Anger-Laden Images of Illness

Since other people cannot easily understand what life is like for ill people, it is inevitable that they at times become sources of frustration and hurt. The woman with multiple sclerosis who complained: "THERE ARE SILLY PEOPLE WHO THINK THEY SHOULD DO EVERYTHING FOR ME" was voicing her irritation at the way she was being treated like a baby when what she wanted was to remain as independent as possible for as long as possible. Another woman with an as yet undiagnosed but debilitating disease resented the pity she experienced from others: "I'M JUST AS LIKELY TO UP AND HIT SOMEONE WHO IS FEELING SORRY FOR ME". A similar misunderstanding of the responses that ill people want from those around them follows: "THEY THINK THEY KNOW WHAT IS BEST FOR YOU, INSTEAD OF LEAVING IT TO YOU TO DECIDE". Sometimes the anger is experienced not so much on one's own behalf but on the behalf of other ill people: "HER HUSBAND IS TERRIBLE. HE GIVES HIS WIFE NO SUPPORT AT ALL". At others it can be directed at groups of which the speaker maybe a member: "DIABETICS AREN'T VERY GOOD TO LIVE WITH AT TIMES. THEY GO OFF INTO MOODS". He is saying, in effect: "These people are irritating; and I am one of them. I am a source of irritation, even to myself".

In our research we have found that hospitalized people express some anger at the health care professionals who work with them. Relatively little of this anger is directed at the more junior staff, such as nurses, who are constantly in contact with them and responsive to their needs. In fact, as is apparent in Chapter 9, much positive feeling is associated with them. Most of the anger is directed at the medical staff who are less readily available and not always able to accomplish their more complex and difficult tasks. These are some of the anger-laden images of "the doctors" which emerged. "I'M DISGUSTED WITH ALL THE DOCTORS. THEY CAN'T FIND OUT WHAT'S WRONG WITH ME". "MY DOCTOR KNOWS NOTHING ABOUT AIDS". "TO BE HONEST WITH YOU, I THOUGHT DR. _____ WAS AN ARROGANT PIG". That note of challenge is sounded again by "I AM GOING TO BATTLE TO GET A SECOND MEDICAL OPINION". Sometimes, however, efforts are made which result only in frustration: "I TRIED TO TELL THE DOCTORS THAT I WAS ALLERGIC TO A LOT OF THINGS AND MIGHT BE TO THEIR NEW DRUG; BUT THEY WOULDN'T LISTEN TO ME".

The unsuccessful efforts described in this statement are also apparent in people's anger-laden images of their illness, such as "I'M VERY FRUSTRATED BECAUSE I CAN'T DO MUCH NOW". This statement by a woman who had recently had a stroke was echoed by a man who had had one heart attack and rehabilitated himself well, only to find himself hit by another: "THIS SECOND ATTACK DESTROYED MY ILLUSIONS". He was finding it difficult to maintain the positive images he had had of his heart being able to regain its functions, in the face of this evidence to the contrary. "I GET ANGRY AND DEPRESSED BY THESE SET-BACKS" presents a similar image.

Many of the people we have interviewed interpret their illness using an image like this: "THE WORST THING IN LIFE IS ILL HEALTH". For them, illness is one of the most difficult things in life to endure. It is not possible for them to imagine anything more distressing than personal illness or injury. They view other people who have retained their health - even those who have lost family, friends or country - as better off than themselves.

Treatments for illness and injury also generate many anger-laden images. Operations, of course, elicit their share of anger. "I'M NOT TOO HAPPY ABOUT THIS OPERATION". "I'VE BEEN TOLD THAT IT'S NOT VERY NICE, COMING OUT OF THE ANAESTHETIC". Some treatments are very unpleasant: "I'D DO ANYTHING RATHER THAN GO THROUGH THE TREATMENT THEY'RE GIVING ME AGAIN". Yet the treatment which generated the most anger is not a physically painful one, but one which may be more psychologically painful - hospitalization. This is often expressed in a straight forward way, for example, "I HATE BEING IN HOSPITAL". Sometimes the almost universal nature of this reaction is observed: "I DON'T SUPPOSE ANYONE COMES INTO HOSPITAL BECAUSE THEY LIKE IT". Actually, there is a small minority of people, who perceive their world outside the hospital as more stressful and unpleasant than that within it, who do not express anger at the hospital. More common, however, are comments such as "I'M BORED IN HERE" and "I DON'T LIKE BEING STUCK IN BED ALL THE TIME".

Other aspects of their lives attract the anger of the severely ill or injured person too. Sometimes this reaction seems to them to be a part of themselves, often a part of them over which they experience very little control: "THESE DAYS I OFTEN GET ANGRY EVEN OVER LITTLE THINGS". The anger seems to ooze out, sometimes in the form of swearing: "IT'S PURE DETERMINATION THAT GETS YOU OUT OF THAT FUCKING WHEELCHAIR". The discontent often seems to be with life in general. "THE DAYS DRAG A BIT". "NOTHING HAPPENS IN MY DULL LIFE". Even personal achievements can invoke anger-laden images: "I LOST WEIGHT THE HARD WAY. I HATED EVERY MINUTE OF IT". Then, too, there is anger directed at the cause of the illness or injury and so at the consequent frustration. "I THINK SOMETHING AT WORK, WHICH I DON'T ENJOY, BROUGHT THIS HEART ATTACK ON". "RUBBISH FOODS CAUSE A LOT OF PROBLEMS, LIKE CANCER". "IF THAT BLOODY RAIN HAD NOT COME PELTING DOWN ALL OF A SUDDEN, I NEVER WOULD HAVE HAD THE ACCIDENT".

Many of the diabetics we have interviewed expressed anger (Viney and Westbrook, 1986). Sometimes it is diffused: "I'M A DIABETIC AND A DAMN GOOD ONE TOO". Some times it represents the frustration induced by their disease: "DIABETES IS A BIT OF A HINDRANCE, A NUISANCE". Insulin injections are often an irritating problem: "YOU DON'T FANCY INJECTING YOURSELF IN OTHER PEOPLE'S HOMES". For some people they remain, after many years of experience with them, an unpleasant and alien burden: "IT'S A VERY UNNATURAL THING TO DO, TO INJECT YOURSELF. IT GOES

AGAINST THE GRAIN". There is also anger about the limitations imposed by the disease: "MY EYES ARE GOING, SO I DON'T LIKE TO DRIVE NOW". A special burden for diabetics seems to be the anger they ascribe to their peculiar physiology rather than to experienced frustration. It is an anger beyond their control: "WHEN MY SUGAR LEVEL GETS HIGH I GET VERY, VERY CANTANKEROUS".

In some situations it can be difficult to express anger directly because of the consequences that people believe may befall. Being hospitalized can be one of those situations. Some people tend more in this direction than others. The statement "I'M NOT A QUARRELSOME PERSON" suggests that the speaker knows what a quarrelsome person is like and knows that she could be one, but refuses to admit it for herself. "IF ANYONE STARTS AN ARGUMENT, I JUST WALK AWAY" is another image based on anger which refuses to acknowledge one's own involvement. Another such statement is one of bland denial: "WE HAVE NO FIGHTS, NO HASSLES". All of the anger implicit here has been relegated to other people. Anger directed at the things in one's world can also be avoided and denied. "I'VE GOT NO COMPLAINTS ABOUT THE HOSPITAL". "THERE'S NOTHING I DON'T LIKE ABOUT BEING HERE". "SINCE I'VE BEEN ILL, LIFE HAS SLOWED DOWN CONSIDERABLY; BUT I DON'T MIND THAT AT ALL".

The Implications of Anger-Laden Images

There is considerably less information available about

anger-laden images of illness than there is about anxiety-laden images. Whether this is because people experience more anxiety than anger or because some researchers have focussed on anxiety to the exclusion of anger, is not yet known. There is evidence of anger associated with illness (Pritchard, 1981), especially if the illness is chronic in its effects (Westbrook and Viney, 1982). There is also evidence of anger associated with disability (Simon, 1971). The more severe the disability, the more anger is likely to be expressed (Viney and Westbrook, 1981a). This finding is similar to that for anxiety-laden images: the more disability is apparent, the more anxiety is to be found.

A variety of diseases very different in their effects have been interpreted using anger-laden images. People with coronary conditions, for example, have shown anger, both when hospitalized immediately after their attack (Hackett, Cassem and Wishnie, 1968) and later at home (Skelton and Dominion, 1973). So have people with cancer (Bard and Sutherland, 1977; Gottschalk and Hoigaard, 1986; Lewis and Bloom, 1978-79; Simonton, Matthews-Simonton and Creighton, 1978), diabetes (Viney and Westbrook, 1986), ulcers (Mlohlen and Brlahler, 1984) and with diseases which cause the nervous system to deteriorate and disabling injuries which result from accidents (Viney, 1972). Anger is also an important component of the psychological reactions of people with AIDS and those who find they are HIV anitbody positive (Faulstich, 1987; Grant and Anns, 1988; Miller and Brown, 1988). Treatments such as hospitalization (Volicer,

1978) and surgery (Weiss, 1969) are also known to elicit anger, as does pain (Khatami and Rush, 1982). So, too, do interpretations of the all-too-possible outcome of severe illness or injury - death. People facing their own death bargain with it, deny it and are depressed by it, but they also become angry about it (Kubler-Ross, 1969; Viney, 1983a). They are angered too by the deaths of others (Bowlby, 1961; Parkes, 1972; Woodfield and Viney, 1985).

If anger can be caused by illness and its implications, to what extent is it a cause of illness? We know that there are ways in which anger can lead to illness. Let us take, as an example, gastrointestinal problems. Anger affects the functioning of the body's autonomic nervous system which, in turn, affects the mobility, secretions, vasoconstriction, vasodilation and excretion of the alimentary canal. If prolonged, anger can interfere with these processes to the point of illness, ranging from minor colonic irritation to perforated ulcers (Heffernon and Lippincott, 1966). Similarly, prolonged wear and tear on the heart muscle can lead to coronary conditions (Haynes et al., 1978). There is also some evidence that anger may be linked with cancer. The form that this relationship appears to take is worthy of note. People have been found to be more likely to develop cancerous growths if they suppress their anger rather than express it (Greer and Morris, 1974; Mahrer, 1980; Temoshek, et al., 1985), and, indeed, to be more vulnerable to physical illness in general (Silverman, 1985). The benefits of recognizing, letting out and using anger will be explored in the next sextion of this chapter.

Before moving to this section, however, it is appropriate to consider whether anger - if it affects the onset of an illness - is related to its progress. Research with cancer patients has revealed the same kind of relationship. It is the people who are aware of and express their anger who survive cancer better than those who suppress it (LeShan, 1977; Stavraky, 1978; Derogatis, Abeloff and Melisaratos, 1979). Work with people suffering a wide range of chronic illness, including heart disease, strokes, degenerative disorders of the nervous system, diabetes, paraplegia and quadraplegia, has confirmed this finding (Viney and Westbrook, 1982c). When people's perceptions of their gains in mobility and relationships with others are compared with their perceptions before the rehabilitation period, much improvement is apparent for those who express their anger directly. Little improvement is found for people who choose to express their anger only indirectly. The results of this study also suggest that those who come to express more anger directly and less indirectly during the period of rehabilitation are most likely to show gains (Viney, in pressa).

Coping with Anger-Laden Images

In this chapter a number of anger-laden images of illness has been described and some explored to give the full flavour of their meaning. Anger directed by people who are ill at both people and things in their world has been considered, as have some images in which the anger is implicit rather than explicit. A sample of anger-laden images from people with diabetes has also been provided. Little is known about which illnesses or injuries are most likely to generate anger; but it is a common reaction to the onset of chronic illness. Anger, at least when it is prolonged and unexpressed, may itself generate illness. Death from cancer, for example, seems more likely to occur if people are not expressing their angry feelings. However, they can be useful when they manifest themselves in a fighting spirit in dealing with the disease process (Watson, et al., 1988). Now an example of a woman whose illness may have been in part due to unrecognized anger is given. Jean T. also shows how the outbursts of hostility she feared (anger of the second kind) were tamed to become incentives for actively exploring her world (anger of the first kind). Ways of recognizing and expressing anger, when alone and with a counsellor, are examined. Finally, how to deal with unavoidable anger and unnecessary frustration is discussed.

Jean had been admitted to hospital for a minor bowel operation, which had to be delayed because of an unexpected rise in her white cell count with no apparent physical cause. For this reason a counsellor was asked to see her. Jean, sitting up very straight in her bed with everything neatly in its place around her, could tell of no psychological, sexual or social problems which might be concerning her. To the psychologist, however, she seemed tightly controlled and somewhat lonely. She saw little of her husband and was visited by no friends while she was in hospital. Mindful of the potential role of anger in her bowel problem (Heffernon and Lippincott, 1966; Bronner-Huszar, 1971), the counsellor invited her to talk about her anger.

Counsellor: "You must be pretty annoyed that no-one has come to visit you yet, Mrs. T.".

Jean: "No... They're probably busy..."

Counsellor: "It's a nuisance having this operation delayed, isn't it?"

Jean (reluctantly): "I suppose so, but it doesn't make any difference to me..."

Jean was not ready to recognize any of her angry feelings. Next day the counsellor tried again.

Counsellor: "Mrs. T., sometimes we feel angry with people and situations but we don't express it because we think something bad might come of it. Angry feelings are good and appropriate feelings to have. I know I would be angry if I had been all ready for an operation and it was suddenly called off..."

Jean: "Well, I'm disappointed not to get it over with, but..."

Counsellor: "What would you say to that haemoglobin count if you had it right there in front of you?"

Jean (giggling): "I don't know... I wish you hadn't come up like this..."

Counsellor: "... You rotten so-and-so! I could have been out of here by now if it hadn't been for you..."

Jean (exploding): "The fucking haemoglobin count loused things up! I worked so hard on getting myself ready for this; and now I have to start all over again".

The counsellor encouraged Jean's expression of her frustration and anger and pointed out to her that its effects were far from catastrophic. Jean came to accept that, just as she needed to be prepared and in control at times, she also needed to let go and let her feelings out. What she had feared as an unstoppable flood of anger was transformed into a controllable urge for exploration which led to some needed changes in her image of herself. Her recovery from surgery was swift.

Ill people can, of course, become aware of their anger-laden images without professional help. Playing with the images which are available as in fantasy or imagination - will often promote such self-awareness (Kelly, 1964; Singer and Pope, 1978). There are questions they can ask themselves which can help to achieve this goal, for example, "When have I been the most angry, in what situation, with whom?". They can set themselves to finish a sentence beginning: "If it weren't for my illness, I...". The answers may surprise them. They can also draw on their imagination to invent a blank movie screen on which they can project shots of people or things that anger them (Shorr, 1972). Imagination can be used, too, to project into the future in order to check out alternative outcomes, for example: "If I let some of my frustration out, what will people do? What will my family do? What will the nurses do? Is there anyone I could share it with, without harming them?".

The keys to coping with anger-laden images are recognizing and expressing the anger contained in them (Greer and Moorey, 1987).

Just shouting, or thumping a pillow, or even cataloguing the crimes of an empty chair which is filled in one's imagination by the person one is angry at (Kempler, 1973) can be helpful. Some people, like Jean, are not initially aware that they are angry. If they want to work alone they should make use of the technique of focussing (Gendlin, 1973). It involves attending to messages from one's body. This is best achieved by providing oneself with privacy and physical comfort, concentrating on the feelings of one's body, trying to describe the qualities of these feelings and working with them while one image emerges clearly (Gendlin, 1981). Although anger may not be what one senses at first, it may be what emerges.

This process can be carried even further with someone who can serve as a counsellor. This person must be prepared to focus entirely on the experience of the ill person and to allow him or her to choose what material is dealt with, at what speed and for how long (Mahrer, 1983). By attending to his or her own bodily feelings during this process, the counsellor will come to share the ill person's experience (Mahrer, 1980b). There was a cancer which was mentioned at the beginning of this chapter, which represented to its host his own potentially explosive violence. For seven years since recognizing and accepting this anger-laden image through this method, he has been cancer-free (Mahrer, 1980a).

Since some frustration is unavoidable, some anger is also unavoidable (Dollard et al., 1939). If this is distressing to people, one way of dealing with it is to practice meditation (Shapiro, 1980). The required state can be achieved in a series of steps which are easy to follow (Rudestam, 1980). It is recognized by an emptying from the mind of all the petty things with which we concern ourselves from day to day. The peace which accompanies this can linger long after each period of meditation has finished. Some of the major frustrations of illness and injury are caused, directly or indirectly, by pain (Cohen and Lazarus, 1979 ; Hamburg, 1974; Miller, 1978; Moos and Tsu, 1977). Meditation has proved to be an effective tool for dealing with pain, at least for those who are experts in its use (Mills and Farrow, 1981).

It is better, of course, to avoid needless frustration. That caused by pain, for example, can often be moderated by relaxation and self-hypnosis as well as by meditation. Methods of dialogue with pain and substituting pleasure for pain have also been developed (Simonton, Matthews-Simonton and Creighton, 1978). These techniques can be learned by people who are in pain and used as adjuncts to analgesics (Noyes, 1981). Other frustrations are often caused for ill and injured people by the people around them, family and friends as well as professional health care givers. Few things are so frustrating to ill people as knowing that they are being talked about behind their back or even in front of them as if they were children (Straus, 1975). Even the most open and trusting of people will become suspicious in these circumstances. It is important to remember that people - whether they be debilitated, in pain or almost comatose - continue to try to make sense of what is happening to them. To render this more difficult for them by deception or withholding information from them is to frustrate them and generate more anger-laden images.

CHAPTER 6

IMAGES OF HELPLESSNESS

"I can't even do my own housework properly."

(Judy C., stroke)

"CANCER CERTAINLY HAS MADE A MESS OF ME." This is the kind of helpless image that experiencing a severe and chronic illness like cancer can lead its sufferers to develop. While people can choose, to some extent, what kind of images they use, certain events can shape so much of their experience that they come to shape their images. Many of the events associated with cancer make people feel powerless in the face of such a force. Cancer attacks people's bodies so effectively that neither those patients nor their medical practitioners can do anything to stop it; and it leaves them in shambles. Yet there is another kind of influence on patients in our health care systems which encourages helpless images. Indeed the images which people are under most pressure to adopt, especially when they are hospitalized, are intrinsically helpless. As one of our informants said: "I'M A GOOD PATIENT. I DO AS I'M TOLD." Why good patients are expected to be obedient is a mystery which will be explored in this chapter.

The only active, constructive human beings for whom goodness is equated with obedience are children. Do people then, become child-like when they become ill? It is believed that they do (Kelly, 1955; Cassell, 1976; Miller, 1978). It seems that, like children, they become more dependent on others: "SOMEONE NOW HAS TO FEED ME MY MEALS." They also lose skills that they had once developed: "I CAN'T EVEN DO MY OWN HOUSEWORK PROPERLY." Many severely ill or disabled people reported feeling helpless in a child-like way. It may be, too, that when adults are ill or injured, because they have relatively few experiences of this kind, they go back to the few relevant images which are available to them. These images are the images of childhood, when illness - albeit often of a minor kind - was almost inevitable. This reaching back for relevant images is not neurotic but realistic. If the images no longer fit well with reality, they can only be improved by experimentation (Kelly, 1969). Since hospital staff are hardly encouraging of experimentation of this kind, it may be they who promote a neurotic regression in patients. People try to avoid feeling helpless (Janis and Rodin, 1979); but that is difficult if they are severely ill and hospitalized.

I will now examine some examples of helpless images. They include images people build to deny that they have any particular intentions or to make explicit their lack of ability. Other forms of helplessness which our informants have mentioned are believing oneself to be influenced more by the physical world of people and objects than it is influenced by oneself. Yet another involves allocating causal roles to it rather than to oneself (Westbrook and Viney, 1980). What is known about helpless images is next examined. There is considerable evidence supporting the view that both illness and hospitalization are fertile grounds for their development. There is also evidence, which I review in this chapter, that images of helplessness can interfere with recovery and rehabilitation. Ways of breaking down the passive, powerless images people who are ill tend to adopt, in order to make way for more assertive, powerful ones are therefore explored.

Some Illness-Related Images of Helplessness

One of the images of helplessness to which our informants have drawn our attention is that which represents their lack of planning or intention. "I JUST LIVE FROM DAY TO DAY. I DON'T THINK ABOUT TOMORROW" is the way some ill people view their lives - an almost complete submission to the illness and what it brings. Others are struck by the uselessness of committing oneself to the future, because of the way severe and unpredictable illness can suddenly destroy that committment: "I CAN'T MAKE ANY LONG RANGE PLANS." Yet others extend this to rule out any committment even to the present. "I HAVE JUST STOPPED LIVING, I GUESS." This withdrawal and passivity is associated with considerable depression. Even this form of helplessness is not so haunting as the images of people who can see no way out, not even by making changes in themselves: "IT'S TOO LATE TO CHANGE NOW." Not to be able to change even oneself is to be helpless indeed.

Not intending to change can be linked with experiencing an inability to change. "YOU CAN'T CHANGE YOUR NATURE." (This belief is very different from mine, which is that we can all change our interpretations and images if we want to). Sometimes ill people feel unable to accomplish things because they are not special kinds of people, not heroes or heroines: "I'M A PRETTY ORDINARY SORT OF

PERSON." Sometimes they feel helpless because, especially if their disease is a progressive one, they may actually be less able as time goes on: "EVERYTHING IS GETTING A BIT TOO MUCH FOR ME." Sometimes it is the effects of their illness or injury which produces such helplessness: "THERE'S NOTHING I CAN DO." A loss of control is perceived, even control of one's normal bodily functions: "IN HOSPITAL ONCE THEY WAKE ME UP, I CAN'T GET BACK TO SLEEP AGAIN. I TOSS AND TURN. I NEVER USED TO BE LIKE THAT."

Many people talk of being influenced by the physical world in which they were living, rather than of themselves influencing it. Pain is, of course, a very common element in helpless images. "AS SOON AS I EAT I GET A FIERCE PAIN IN MY STOMACH." "I ADJUSTED TO THE PAIN BEFORE THE OPERATION. I'LL JUST HAVE TO ADJUST TO THIS." "I SUFFER FROM NERVES IN MY BACK." Sometimes it is the general state of their bodies which makes them feel so helpless, "IT'S MY HEALTH THAT IS HOLDING ME BACK" or "THIS STROKE HAS REALLY SLOWED ME DOWN." They also fear the future: "I DREAD BEING TERRIBLY ILL AND BED-RIDDEN." It can also be the specific symptoms of their illness which render them helpless. As one man said of the emphysema which was making it increasingly difficult for him to breath: "IT'S A VERY SIMILAR THING TO DROWNING ON DRY LAND."

Treatments for illnesses and injuries can render people helpless too. "I'VE GOT TO LOSE WEIGHT." "I'M NOT ALLOWED TO TAKE

ANOTHER DRINK FOR THE REST OF MY LIFE." "I REALISE THAT THIS SURGERY HAS GOT TO BE DONE BUT..." So can being in hospital. "IT JUST DRIVES ME CRAZY SITTING HERE DOING NOTHING ALL DAY." "YOU'RE TIED DOWN IN HOSPITAL." "IT'S LIKE BEING IN A PRISON." With the best of intentions, family and staff can also add to people's images of helplessness: "THERE'S NOTHING WORSE THAN BEING MADE TO FEEL TOTALLY USELESS."

Helplessness has also been apparent in images which involve believing the physical world to be the prime cause of events rather than their being amenable to one's own control. Ill people sometimes regard their physical characteristics, such as sex or stage of the lifespan, as such causes, "I'M GETTING VERY MOODY. I THINK IT'S MY AGE", thereby relieving the speaker of any responsibility for her irritability. Sometimes they experience themselves as involved in some vast and continuing process which they cannot control, and which is mechanical in nature: "I FEEL THAT I'M PART OF A MACHINE WHICH HAS STARTED UP IN THE HOSPITAL AND WILL JUST PICK ME UP AND PROCESS ME THROUGH WHEN IT'S READY. NO! I CAN'T BACK OUT OF THE SURGERY NOW." Sometimes God replaces the machine: "I JUST ACCEPT WHATEVER THE LORD'S WILL IS FOR ME NOW." It can, however, be to the patron saint of gamblers, Lady Luck, that people consign causality. "I WAS VERY LUCKY TO PULL THROUGH." "MY HUSBAND WAS VERY GOOD ABOUT MY MASTECTOMY SCARS. I WAS LUCKY."

Our informants have also expressed helplessness in ways which show that they are aware of making an effort and persisting in what they are trying to do, but not having much success. The lady who, while in hospital, suffered a severe allergic reaction to the drugs given her by the medical staff, provides a good example: "I TRIED TO TELL THE DOCTORS I HAD ALLERGIES, BUT NOBODY WOULD LISTEN TO ME." Other examples have been provided by stroke victims who were struggling to cope with their paralysis: "IT'S TERRIBLY DIFFICULT NOW SHOWERING AND DRESSING" and "GETTING ABOUT IS PRETTY DIFFICULT." There are also people who know what they want but cannot achieve it and who then feel helpless. "I CAN'T GO OUT WHEN I WANT TO." "I CAN'T DO THE WORK I WANT TO DO."

Some diabetics develop many helpless images (Viney and Westbrook, 1986). Even being told they have diabetes is "LIKE SOME-ONE DELIVERING A BLOW TO YOUR SOLAR PLEXIS." The wind is knocked out of them. They tend to see its occurrence as due to pressures from the outside world: "IT WAS BROUGHT ON BY STRESS." They are struck by how much it affects their day-to-day living. "THE DIABETES CERTAINLY DOES CHANGE YOUR LIFE AROUND." "THE MOST DIFFICULT THING ABOUT THE PROBLEM OF DIABETICS IS THAT THEY CAN'T HAVE AS MUCH OF A LIFE AS OTHER PEOPLE CAN." Many things about it make life difficult for them. "YOU WANT TO DO THINGS BUT YOU FEEL TOO TIRED TO DO THEM." "THE NEEDLES HURT LIKE ANYTHING! DON'T LET

ANY BODY TELL YOU DIFFERENT." "YOU HAVE TO BE CAREFUL OF HAVING HYPOS." There are also diabetics who are especially aware of the unpredictable course of their disease: "I AM A BRITTLE DIABETIC - AN UNCONTROLLABLE DIABETIC." Diabetes seems to be, for those who have to deal with its effects on their bodies, an over-whelmingly powerful factor in their lives.

The Implications of Images of Helplessness

Helplessness is experienced by ill people, as we have seen, as their own lack of planning and intentions, as well as of ability. It can also take the form of perceiving the physical world as more powerful, that is, more influential and more likely to be the cause and origin of events, than oneself. Sometimes images of helplessness have the theme of trying to do something but not succeeding. At others, the dominating theme is knowing what one wants to do but not being able to do it. People dealing with diabetes painted these images vividly. Now some of their implications will be examined. Being ill and disabled encourages such helplessness, as do the routines peculiar to hospitals. The most important implications of images of helplessness, however, are seen in their influence on patients' rehabilitation and recovery.

Helplessness and dependency are integral parts of the world of ill people who have been hospitalized (Cassell, 1976; Peterson and Raps, 1984; Viswanathan and Vizner, 1984). Together with the loss of the sense of their own indestructability and the sudden shrinkage of their world to include only the hospital ward, these are two of the most striking features of ill peoples' interpretations of what is happening to them (Viney, 1980). Together with anxiety-laden images, these images are important features of peoples' initial reaction to chronic illness (Cantor, 1986; LeShan, 1977; Westbrook and Viney, 1980). There is evidence that these images are used by people with cardiac conditions (Viswanathan and Vizner, 1984), spinal cord injuries (Shadish, Hickman and Arrick, 1981), and recurrent genital herpes (Silver et al., 1986), as well as those in pain (Khatami and Rush, 1982; Raps et al., 1982; Turk, Meichenbaum and Genest, 1983). Like anxiety-laden images, helpless images are more likely to become important if people have more severe disabilities (Viney and Westbrook, 1981a). They can also become important when treatment stops (Abrams and Finesinger, 1953).

It may be that it is not only illness which encourages images of helplessness, but the hospitalization which often accompanies it (Volicer, 1978). The organization, personnel hierarchy and routinization of the hospital can all be seen as factors which strip power from ordinary, ill people (Taylor, 1979; Anderson, 1981). These people are sometimes discussed by health care personnel as if they do not exist, except as a malfunctioning arm, leg or heart (Straus, 1975). They are often provided with very little information with which to make decisions (Volicer, 1978). Perhaps this is because of the authoritarian attitudes the staff sometimes take towards patients and their illness (Kinsman et al., 1976; Janis and Rodin, 1979). Many physicians conceive of health care as a process of social influence with themselves as the influencer (Friedman and Di Matteo, 1979). The traditional view of the relationship between physician and patient is one in which the patient is passive (Szasz and Hollender, 1956). The very title of "patient", one who is long-suffering and forebearing, contributes to these images of helplessness. However, while these influences during hospitalization may be important, chronically ill people have been found to continue to use them after discharge (Westbrook and Viney, 1980). Of course, when their illness is chronic, discharge from hospital has not secured their discharge from the "patient" role.

This is unfortunate; since there is ample evidence that helpless images of illness are associated with poor rehabilitation and recovery. For example, more passive coping with their disability and treatment by people with severe burns has been found in those who recover from those burns more slowly and less completely than those who are more active (Andreasen et al ., 1972). People with cancer who tend to see the people and events of their physical world as determining their fate do not adjust so well to their illness as do those who view themselves as the most important influence in their lives (Worden and Sobel, 1978), and their illness is more likely to have a poor outcome (Greer, Morris and Pettingale, 1982). Similarly, people with a range of chronic illnesses who use many such images show little rehabilitation later when compared with those who use fewer of them (Viney and Westbrook, 1982c). Effective rehabilitation has been shown to include an increase in peoples' images of control and competence, as well as a decline in their images of helplessness (Albrecht and Higgens, 1977). Ill and injured people who do not experience such helplessness are more likely to be involved in successful rehabilitation (Shontz, 1975), including showing more gains from treatment for chronic pain (Chapman and Brena, 1982).

This may be because images of helplessness not only make rehabilitation difficult but because they can, themselves, lead to illness. In their extreme form they involve a sense of psychological impotence, a feeling of being unable to cope with changes in one's world and a recognition that one's own means of coping no longer seem to work (Seligman and Garber, 1980). They can lead to people "giving up", which in turn is said to lead to increased vulnerability to disease and even to death (Hutschnecker, 1981; Schmale, 1972; Weisman and Worden, 1975). Researchers in the field are coming to accept that this is so (Antonovsky, 1979; Cohen, 1979), perhaps because of the evidence available which suggests that identifying people using helpless images may be an effective aid in predicting cancer (Schmale and Iker, 1971). People using such images may also be more vulnerable to the illness-provoking effects of stress to which I referred in Chapter 4 (Johnson and Sarason, 1978; Matheny and Cupp, 1983).

Coping with Images of Helplessness

Many of the different meanings of helplessness have been explored in this chapter, all of them relating to a sense of powerlessness in the face of illness-related events. The child-like nature of the "patient" role has been noted. So have its temptation to regress to dependency and its manifestation in forms such as perceived deficiencies in planning, in general ability, incapacity to influence and in a tendency to be overwhelmed by other people and events. People do not like to feel helpless. This is just as well; because their choice of helplessness images may be associated not only with slower recovery from illness and poor rehabilitation, but with the onset of illness and even death. There is a good reason, then, to want to change these images. Some suggestions for doing so follow. They are based on the evidence available that helpless images in the ill can be changed (Forester, Kornfeld and Fleiss, 1982; Viney, Benjamin and Preston, in pressa; Viney et al., 1985). They include some physical exercises and some ways in which hospitalization, and health care in general, can work for rather than against these changes. Specific examples of hospital-based techniques are examined, together with techniques of more general application, such as assertiveness training and fixed role therapy. An account of a therapeutic interaction between a counsellor and a woman with some disruptive and distressing images of helplessness is also provided.

When I contemplate doing one of my favourite physical exercises for dispelling helpless images I realized how strong the constraints of the "patient" role are. The exercise consists of taking a breath of air and then exhaling as long and as deeply as possible, slapping one's chest vigorously and yelling "Ahhhhh" loudly. This is followed by a very deep intake of breath which is held again as long as possible. The result is a feeling of power and exhilaration. Perhaps that is why it is so difficult to imagine doing it in the surgery of a medical practitioner or on a hospital ward. This exercise can, however, be carried out to good effect elsewhere.

A form of stress innoculation has been developed with the aim of changing helpless people into resourceful people (Meichenbaum, 1977). This techniques has much in common with rational-emotive therapy (Ellis, 1984; Grieger, 1985). It focusses on their appraisal of the events with which they have to deal and of their own capacity to cope with them, their learning and trying out of new skills. That appraisal is, of course, carried out using images of oneself in relation to events. Different images are useful at different stages of the coping process. During preparation, these kinds of images work against helpless images: "I CAN DEVELOP A PLAN. I'LL JUST THINK ABOUT IT FIRST. I FEEL ANXIOUS BECAUSE I WANT TO DO WELL, AND THAT'S IN MY FAVOUR". During the actual event, these images will be effective: "I'M IN CONTROL. ONE STEP AT A TIME. I CAN DO IT. MY ANXIETY IS A WAY OF REMINDING ME THAT I AM MAKING A BIG EFFORT". There are images, too, that can deal effectively with feelings of being overwhelmed: "I'LL JUST DEAL WITH THE HERE AND NOW. IT WILL BE OVER SOON". There are also self-congratulatory images that underline one's successes: "I DID IT! IT GETS EASIER EVERY TIME!". All of these images of competence can become available to ill people who are feeling helpless, if they choose to use them.

While hospitalization makes it difficult to expel helpless images in this way, because it is a new and different situation for people it can be used by them as an opportunity for change (Viney, et al., 1985 a; b). It is easier for people to change if they are away from many of the cues which prompt them to use the same means of coping they have used before (Kelly, 1955). It is also easier for them to change when they are not continually surrounded by people with whom they have already developed relationships so that these people have certain expectations of them. What can be very helpful in attempts to get rid of some helpless images while in hospital is having access to someone, a professional counsellor or any other staff member with sufficient time available, who is new to the person but can "give permission" for attempts to change and be responsive and approving when some change is accomplished. In that way a new but trusting relationship can be established which enables and rebuilds their illness-related images (Fransella, 1987) and allows people to test their new skills (Hobson, 1985). Family and friends can help with these tasks, too, by being accepting and supporting of any attempts by the ill person to be less helpless.

Other useful ways of dealing with helpless images come from the cognitive-behavioural approach to illness (Moorey and Greer, 1987). Taking over the control in the relationship between patient and health professional is one such method. People who are ill do choose whether to comply with the treatment offered or not. They can also choose to work on keeping the parts of their bodies not affected by the illness or injury as healthy and functioning as well as possible, and banish their helpless images by success in this area. Recognizing that control, especially of illness, is not all-or-none but a matter of degree can be helpful, as can establishing control over other areas of their lives, such as family and friends or work. Those experiences intrinisic to being seriously ill, such as waiting for appointments and transport, which are also fraught with helplessness, can be modified by effectively predicting them and planning strategies to deal with them.

One important source of helplessness for newly hospitalized patients is the disorientation and dislocation of being in an alien environment, in which the sights, smells and sounds are not familiar and even the rules governing day-to-day routines have changed. The uncertainty generated by this lack of information can be dealt with by gaining that information, as described in Chapter 3. People who see themselves as helpless, however, extend this image well into their hospital stay. They feel helpless about their illness and its treatment. They feel helpless, also, about maintaining their right of access to information about their illness and its treatment and are timid about asking the medical staff questions about them. The images they build up, therefore, as well as being helpless, tend to be poorly informed and so discrepant with those of others; and they become a continuing source of anxiety and frustration.

The case of Elizabeth S. demonstrates this. She had been hospitalized as the result of a car accident. Her recovery was taking six to seven months, although none of her multiple leg fractures was very serious. She had achieved few rehabilitation goals. She described herself as "a good patient", using the passive image which was explored earlier in this chapter. She acknowledged feeling helpless but was not aware of any anxiety. She did become aware of it, however, when she was suddenly removed to an isolation ward because of infection. It was then that she asked to see a counsellor, who helped her to express her feelings and to secure information about the hospital hierarchy so that she could enquire about her disabilities and rehabilitation.

Counsellor: "What's wrong, Mrs. S.?"

Elizabeth (crying): "I've been stuck in here and they're treating me like a leper. I don't know what's going on. They just come and got me in the middle of the night and wheeled me in here. The nurse wouldn't say anything..."

Counsellor: "Just what did they tell you Mrs. S.? Nurse must have said something."

Elizabeth: "She said I had an infection but wouldn't say anything else. Everyone who comes in here - I ask them but they won't tell me. And now they must be angry with me because hardly anyone comes in here to see me."

Counsellor: "I don't think they are angry. When one patient gets an infection they have to make sure that the other patients are protected from it. Even the staff can carry it around on their clothes. So they follow a routine in which few staff members come in contact with an infected person."

Elizabeth: "Well, how can I find out what is going on? My doctor isn't coming in Monday, so I can't see him. And I can't get up and ring my family..."

Counsellor: "It feels awful to be helpless doesn't it. The hospital has another routine which won't let the nurses tell you. But you will need to get one of them to ring your doctor for you; and he can get a resident to talk to you today."

Elizabeth (still crying): "Oh I couldn't do that. Anyway they won't take any notice of me."

Counsellor: "Yes they will. When you've cried enough to feel better, I'll show you how to arrange it."

Eventually, Elizabeth risked a timid request and was able to secure the information she wanted. From this small beginning, she was able to go on to increase her role as a participant in her own treatment while still in hospital and later at home.

One of the techniques used later with Elizabeth which aided her in getting rid of her helpless images was assertiveness training. This is a procedure which helps people to learn to ask directly for what they want, rather than being inhibited by anxiety or guilt or side-tracked by frustration and anger. Several accounts of the steps involved are available (Rimm and Masters, 1979; Tasto and Skjei, 1979; Wolpe, 1973). The first step consists of identification of situations in which people find if difficult to make their needs clear to others. They usually also learn to use relaxation techniques at this point. Then they go on to imagine themselves being assertive in those situations, using relaxation as a counter to any interfering anxiety which may arise. There are also rehearsals with the others, including some reversal of roles so as to find out what it is like to try to respond to someone who is blocked from asserting themselves. Finally, the assertive techniques which have been learned are tried in the situations which were initially identified as problem situations.

A similar technique which ill and hospitalized people with helpless images can use for themselves to good effect is fixed role therapy (Bonarius, 1970; Karst and Trexler, 1970). Although one can always talk to oneself or other people about becoming competent and in control rather than helpless, to act out these images is much more effective than to merely talk about them (Radley, 1974). Getting rid of helpless images can best be accomplished by putting other, incompatible ones in their place. This can be achieved by a technique which involves acting out a fixed role, like a part in a play. The images of this role should include those which one would like to apply to oneself but does not. For maximum effect it should be played, not only with one's counsellor and then with one's health professionals but also in imagination at least with one's parents (Epting and Nazario, 1987). The person feeling helpless therefore includes in the role description themes like these: "X is a competent person who is able to be open and friendly with people. X feels in control of situations and well able to deal with anything that comes up." Even though helpless people find this role to be alien to them, they can put it on like a mask and try it out in various situations. They soon learn that they can, while acting out the role, be assertive. And if they can be assertive when playing a part, why not when they are themselves? The immediate rewards inherent in this experience of oneself as assertive also help to banish images of helplessness and keep them at bay.

CHAPTER 7

DEPRESSION-LADEN IMAGES

"My depression is a lot harder to cope with

than my illness is."

(John W., multiple sclerosis)

Evidence of depression-laden images among ill and injured people has not been difficult to find. Often their statements about these images are simple and yet far-reaching in their implications. "I OFTEN FEEL DEPRESSED" is one such comment. People who make such a statement know how it is to feel trapped and yet unwanted, hopeless and yet deprived. They must also know what it is like not to feel these emotions - to feel free, wanted, hopeful and fulfilled. But their statement implies that they experience that first set of feelings more frequently than the second. Another similar comment which is made often by ill people is "MY DEPRESSION IS A LOT HARDER TO COPE WITH THAN MY ILLNESS IS." For these people, the feeling of entrapment extends beyond the immediate effects of their physical problems to engulfment by their depressive feelings about it. Physical disability, pain and the stresses of hospitalization might all be dealt with; depression-laden images are feared more. Patients making this statement have developed some confidence in their ability to deal effectively with their illness but not with those images.

Constriction of images, especially of images of oneself, is common among people who feel depressed (Rowe, 1978). "I AM USELESS", for example, is an image of oneself which effectively reduces the demands people can make of themselves. Some depressed people are aware of the ways in which they reduce their own choices. People who say, for example, "I LOCK MYSELF IN TOO MUCH EMOTIONALLY" are aware of the restrictions they place on themselves as far as feeling is concerned. This self-constriction can eventually lead to the pessimism, lack of flexibility and ruling out of choices involved in a statement like: "I FEEL TRAPPED." Such constriction is often to be seen in people who are mourning the loss of a loved one (Woodfield and Viney, 1985). It is also likely to occur when sick and injured people are mourning their lost or damaged body parts or the life style of which they have been deprived (Adams and Lindemann, 1974).

In this chapter I examine some of the most common depression-laden images of illness. These images include elements of hopelessness, deprivation, embarrassment and guilt. Images involving embarrassment and shame are given from our interviews with women who have had mastectomies because of possible breast cancer. For these women such images are very vivid. Similarly, guilt-dominated images of illness are drawn from some diabetic patients who have spoken to us, for whom they are especially important. Once the value of these images is clear, some of the ways in which they can influence how people live their lives is dealt with: how they recur as a reaction to illness but can continue for a long time, how they can generate illness and affect recovery. Finally, suggestions are made about how to cope with depression-laden images.

Some Depression-Laden Images of Illness

Hopelessness, deprivation, embarrassment and guilt are the dominant themes of the depressive images of illness which people construct. Here are some hopeless images. "IF YOU ARE NOT HEALTHY, NOTHING SEEMS VERY BRIGHT." "I JUST SIT AT HOME MOST OF THE TIME, FEELING SORRY FOR MYSELF." "YOU FEEL SAD WHEN YOU REALISE THAT THINGS AREN'T EVER GOING TO BE ANY DIFFERENT." "IF YOU START FEELING SORRY FOR YOURSELF, YOU CAN GET REALLY DOWN." "THINGS ARE GETTING WORSE AS I GET OLDER." "I HAVE LOST ALL INTEREST IN LIFE." "AIDS IS AFFECTING ME IN SO MANY WAYS NOW, I CAN ONLY SEE DEATH ENDING IT".

Each hopeless image can be examined in more detail too, as these examples show. "THERE IS NO CURE FOR WHAT I'VE GOT" reflects an image which recognizes that, while in the twentieth century some illnesses can be cured, this cessation of symptoms and subsequent return to the old life style is not believed to be possible for the person making such a statement. The statements by another speaker acknowledge an even further reaching form of hopelessness: "I CAN'T THINK ABOUT THE FUTURE. I MIGHT BE DISAPPOINTED AGAIN". They are based on an image constructed through failure after failure, blow after blow. They represent a depth of hopelessness in which the image-maker constricts his world to the present and the past alone.

Deprivation is another theme which characterizes depression-laden images of illness. Sometimes the deprivation refers to a lack of interpersonal support, of rewarding relationships with others, for example, "I SEE NO LIVING SOUL FOR DAYS ON END" and "THE FAMILY DON'T COME TO SEE ME VERY OFTEN". The social isolation that stems from this kind of depression I deal with in Chapter 8. More often, people are experiencing deprivation of different kinds. "IT TAKES HALF THE PLEASURE OUT OF LIFE WHEN YOU CAN NO LONGER DO YOUR OWN SHOPPING". "I HAVE NO RECENT MEMORY AT ALL. IT IS HARD TO LIVE WITH THAT". "I HAVE TO HAVE SOMEONE WITH ME 24 HOURS A DAY; SO I DON'T GET MUCH PRIVACY". Privacy seems relatively unimportant to those of us who can have it when we want it. When people are severely disabled by injury or progressive disease they often have to live out every aspect of their lives under the never-ending scrutiny of family and health professionals as well as other patients.

Embarrassed images of illness are also common, especially when peoples' self-esteem is slipping because of their disabilities. "I'M NOT COPING TERRIBLY WELL WITH THE HOSPITAL". "AFTER THE OPERATION, I'M AFRAID I WON'T BE ABLE TO DO MUCH FOR A WHILE". "I GET A BIT EMOTIONAL THESE DAYS". "IT MAY MEAN I WILL BE A BURDEN TO MY FAMILY". "YOU JUST FEEL SO USELESS". Low self-esteem is characteristic of depression in many situations (Beck, 1967). These images of inadequacy and embarrassment occur when people recognize that they are interacting with others in ways which do not fit with others' expectations of them (McCoy, 1977). This theme is especially apparent in these two examples. One statement was made by a man with multiple sclerosis who was rapidly losing control over his muscles: "I DON'T FEEL LIKE THE HEAD OF THE HOUSEHOLD ANY MORE". The other was made by a man who, after a gall bladder operation, needed to be fed intravenously. His veins were small and hard to find; and the probing of relays of nurses caused him so much pain that tears came to his eyes. His comment on this was: "I DON'T CRY IN PUBLIC. EVEN WHEN MY WIFE DIED I DIDN'T DO THAT".

One group of people who express many images of shame and embarrassment are the women who have had mastectomies. They are aware of the changes to their physical appearance made by the loss or partial loss of a breast and many doubt their continuing attractiveness as women. This is so with that most important man in their lives, "WHEN I FIRST HAD MY BREAST OFF, I WOULDN'T LET MY HUSBAND SEE ME WITH NO CLOTHES ON" and with people with whom they make only occasional contact, "I WAS EMBARRASSED WHEN I WENT OUT WITH PEOPLE WHO KNEW I HAD HAD A MASTECTOMY". Even women who want other women to know that they can survive cancer of the breast, and so let it be widely known that they have had a mastecomy, find it a cause for shame: "I FIND IT HARD TO COPE WITH THE LOOK ON PEOPLES' FACES WHEN YOU TELL THEM". Some women deny these feelings, "BEING DISFIGURED DOESN'T WORRY ME"; but most of them experience times when their self-esteem is at a very low ebb, "IF I'M ON A DOWN DAY, I JUST PUSH THE MIRROR TO ONE SIDE SO I DON'T HAVE TO SEE MYSELF".

Guilty feelings, too, arise when people realise that there is a gap between image and reality. It is people's recognition that they are not interacting with others in ways which fit with their most important expectations of themselves that leads to their feeling guilty (Kelly, 1955). A woman who had lived a healthy and hectic life with her large and happy family until she suffered a stroke illustrates this. She saw herself as the care-giver in the family, the one concerned about everyone else. She could not fit her new role in the family with her old expectations of herself. "I'M ALWAYS THINKING ABOUT ME. I'VE NEVER BEEN LIKE THAT BEFORE. I FEEL AS THOUGH EVERYTHING REVOLVES AROUND ME. I FEEL GUILTY ABOUT THAT". Other failures to meet one's own expectations about which patients felt guilty included avoiding surgery, "I JUST LET IT GO AND LET IT GO" and continuing to smoke, "I SHOULD GIVE IT UP, I KNOW". There are also expectations not directly related to illness but called into question by it, such as those about close family relationships: "MY SISTER HASN'T BEEN TO SEE ME SINCE I'VE BEEN IN HOSPITAL. OF COURSE I HAVEN'T SPOKEN TO HER IN FIVE YEARS. IT'S NOT NICE FOR SISTERS TO FIGHT, IS IT..."

One group of patients using many guilt-laden images are the diabetics (Viney and Westbrook, 1986). "I SHOULD HAVE LOOKED AFTER MYSELF MORE". They are concerned especially with their dietary restrictions which they often couch as if they were moral injunctions: "YOU'VE GOT TO DO THE RIGHT THING WHEN YOU EAT, LIKE YOU'VE GOT TO EAT YOUR MEALS ON TIME" and "YOU'VE GOT TO CUT YOUR SWEET STUFF DOWN". So many diabetics admit: "I KEEP EATING FOODS I SHOULDN'T BE". One of their most depression-laden images of diabetes represents it as an arbiter of right and wrong, an awful judge whose anger they arouse by their all too human liking for sweets.

The Implications of Depression-Laden Images

According to the research which has been reported, images involving hopelessness, deprivation, shame and guilt are often constructed by ill people in order to make sense of illness-related events (Abram, 1972; Rodin and Voshart, 1986; Viney, 1980), especially if they are hospitalized or the illness is chronic (Fava et al., 1984; Garron and Leavitt, 1983) This appears to be true for diabetic patients (Engelmann, 1976; Skenazy and Bigler, 1985; Viney and Westbrook, 1986), and also for cancer patients (Bard and Sutherland, 1977; Craig and Abeloff, 1974; Gottschalk and Hoigaard, 1986; Hughson et. al., 1986; Lewis and Bloom, 1978-79; Maguire et al., 1978). This has not always proved to be the case (Plumb and Holland, 1977). There is evidence from many cultures that people who have had heart attacks use many depression-laden images shortly afterwards (Dorossiev, Paskova and Zachariev, 1976; Hackett, Cassem and Wishnie, 1968; Stocksmeier, 1976). These images may be triggered by a variety of events (Sachar, 1975). Coronary patients do not necessarily produce more depressive images than people with other kinds of chronic diseases (Kiecolt-Glaser and Williams, 1987; McIvor, Riklan and Reznikoff, 1984; Manne and Sandler, 1984). Indeed, if the illness which is being coped with involves long-term disability rather than a brief period of incapacity, it is the severity of that disability which determines the extent of the depression-laden images (Viney and Westbrook, 1981a; Hlatky et al., 1986), together with the attendant pain (Keefe et al., 1986; Khatami and Rush, 1982).

Those images can be quite long-lasting and wide-spread. The most extensive research bearing on this statement has dealt with people who have had heart attacks. For them these depression-laden images persist much longer than would have been expected if they were part of an immediate reaction to the attack. They tend to continue after people have been discharged from hospital and even increase at that time (Hackett and Cassem, 1975). Like anxiety-laden images, depression-laden images have been shown to linger for as long as 15 months after discharge (Rodda, Miller and Bruhn, 1971). They can be generated by improvements as well as declines in health (Shontz, 1977). They can appear at the end of treatment (Holland et al., 1979). Depression-laden images can spread, too, in an almost contagious way to people in contact with others who are using them. Wives of cardiac patients, for example, have been shown to employ them during the convalescence of their husband (Skelton and Dominian, 1973).

Depressive images like other negative images, occur not only as a consequence of illness but may even be a contributing cause (Gunderson and Rahe, 1974). If this is so, then the cross-cultural findings of such images in people dealing with AIDS (Dilley et al., 1985; Miller and Brown, 1988; Viney et al., 1987) is of great concern as it is for any illness. The evidence in support of this view is as yet incomplete. One supporting study has found that nursing students who mention many depressive themes during an interview miss classes because of illness and visit the available health care facilities more often than those who use few (Cleghorn and Streiner, 1979). It may be, not so much that depressed people are more often ill, but that people who are unhappy focus more on their minor physical symptoms than those who are happily occupied with other things (Mechanic, 1974).

Any causal relationships between depression-laden images and ill health are difficult to tease out. The relationships which images of shame and guilt bear to different aspects of illness testify to this. In one study health care professionals were asked to judge the extent of the observable disabilities of a group of chronically ill people. These people were also asked to assess, for themselves, the extent of their handicaps. Severity of observed disability proved to be related to the prevalence of shame-laden images; severity of handicap, as it was perceived by the chronically ill person, was related to the prevalence of guilt-laden images (Viney and Westbrook, 1984). Whether greater perceived handicap causes more guilt-laden images, or whether guilt, generated by unmet expectations, causes handicaps to be peceived as greater, it is too early to tell. Both statements may be true for different people at different times.

Nor can we yet be sure about the effects of depressive illness-related images on the people who construct them. Researchers, again working with people with heart conditions, have found them to be associated with more complicated recovery while in hospital (Pancheri, et al., 1978) and with a lower chance of survival after a heart attack (Bruhn, Chandler and Wolf, 1969) or with cancer (Weisman and Worden, 1975). Yet depressive images have also been linked with longer survival of coronary disease (Henrichs, McKenzie and Almond, 1969) and of cancer (Derogatis, Abeloff and Melisaratos, 1979). Accident victims who have been rendered paraplegic or quadraplegic have been found to cope better if they blame themselves for their accidents rather than others, that is, if their interpretations of what has happened to them make use of images dominated by guilt and shame (Bulman and Wortman, 1977). This has been found to be true for cancer patients too (Worden and Sobel, 1978). Although the evidence is not yet all in, it suggests on balance that depression-laden images may be necessary and their expression helpful to people who are ill or injured.

Coping with Depression-Laden Images

Whether these images are helpful or not, they are inherently distressing to the people whose imagined worlds they dominate. By their very nature, they are constricting and deprive people of choices

(Neimeyer, 1985). They make the life of people using them seem meaningless and lacking in purpose. For these reasons it is useful to know how to change and reinterpret depression-laden images. Ways of dealing with images of hopelessness, deprivation, shame and guilt will be examined, including some techniques which have beem effectively used by patient, patients' family and friends or health care professionals (Forester, Kornfeld and Fleiss, 1982; Viney, Benjamin and Preston, in pressd; Viney et al.,1987a). I shall also provide an example of a facilitating interaction with a depressed man who had recently experienced his first heart attack.

Ill people should be encouraged to accept and explore their depression-laden images. Trying to ignore them or to hide them from others merely takes up more energy, so that people feel drained and so more depressed than before. Ill people can do much to break down their own depression-laden images. They can, for example, keep records of their changes of mood and so identify some of the events which build up and break down these images (Tasto and Skjei, 1979). They can attend to the content of these images and to the assumptions on which they are based and evaluate the evidence relating to such assumptions (Tarrier and McGuire, 1984; Turk and Rennert, 1981). "IF ANYTHING GOES WRONG, IT IS MY FAULT", for example, is a depressive image which can quickly be disconfirmed by careful observation of events. There are, inevitably, many times when things "go wrong" when it is someone else's fault or no-one's fault at all. Those who are depressed can also work to improve their relationships with a variety of people and so add to and strengthen the sources of social support available to them (Tasto and Skjei, 1979).

Much of the influence of depressive images can be reduced when they are shared with others (Miller, 1986). This does not mean that someone listening to ill or injured people talk of their hopelessness should let himself or herself be overcome by those images too; but he or she should listen well enough to be able to understand them. Once that is achieved it is appropriate to confront some of those images with more hopeful interpretations of events. Ill people can also be helped to construct more positive images by focussing on those things in life which they have enjoyed in the past and which they can enjoy in their imaginings now (Beck, 1967). These can include people, objects, ideas or activities which require physical effort of them are particularly useful in dealing with depressive images. Some of these sources of enjoyment are bound to be still available to them; and recognition of this can be one of the first steps out of their entrapment. It also provides reassurance (Beck, Emery and Greenberg, 1985).

Images of deprivation also need to be dealt with. These images of loss are often similar to those constructed by people who have lost some person close to them (Epting and Neimeyer, 1984). The extent to which mourning is fully carried out, whether it be of person or life style, depends on the flexibility of the mourners' sets of images and the ways in which they help them understand what they are experiencing. If people find it easy to make sense of illness-related events, they will be able eventually to complete their mourning process and move on to some enjoyment of their new life style (Woodfield and Viney, 1985). If they are not able to do so, their mourning will be prolonged; and they will continue to be trapped by their depression. Often depression-laden images have been built up by them because of the speed and impact of illness-related events like a heart attack. Taking time to sort them out and to interpret them, both introspectively and with the aid of a good listener, can be very helpful.

The images people build up to represent themselves determine how they act (Kelly, 1955). This is why it is important to help ill or injured people to deal with their images of shame and guilt. Shameful images, especially, suggest a poor view of oneself and low self-esteem. There is a technique, rather like the one discussed in relation to hopelessness, which can be used here. It encourages people to consider their own good qualities. Many of the stroke patients who have talked with us, for example, have felt useless and embarrassed because of their paralysis. Their initial reaction to this technique is often to say "I couldn't do that" or "I don't have any." Persistence with the request, however, eventually leads to recognition of some pre-stroke images of themselves of which they are proud. Perhaps more important is the recognition by these people who have been severely disabled by strokes that they still retain strengths which can be put to good use.

Guilt-laden images can be similarly hurtful to people who are ill. Once they have been recognized and explored by patients it is then possible to go on to reconstruct these images, or to find alternative images to take their place. These image changes can be experimentally tried out with a counsellor; but eventually they will need to be practised with family and friends. An example of such counselling with Richard W., a 46 year old army sergent, shows how this can occur. Richard, who was married and the father of two boys, had been hospitalized because of a heart attack. He carried out the duties of his army post with great care and precision; and the image of himself, both on the job and at home, as a strong, even heroic man was very important to him. The guilt generated by his attack was apparent in the regime he intended to lay down for himself when he left the hospital. He was going to deprive himself of so many forms of enjoyment: "I should eat and drink less. I should smoke less. I should have less sex." It was as if he was punishing himself for his sins.

The dialogue which follows shows how he came to recognize his guilt-laden images. He was constructing these images because he felt he was not meeting his expectations of himself. It took place after he had been discharged from hospital but had been readmitted on the evening of the same day because of anginal pain. Clinging to his image of himself as a strong man, he had sat up for six hours at home to receive visitors and then, finally in bed, he had become sexually aroused with his wife.

Counsellor: "Last time we talked it was about how strong and brave men have to be in our society. Do you think this had anything to do with what happened when you went home?"

Richard: "I've been thinking about that. I was wrong to stay up so long, I know."

Counsellor: "Do you think that might have been because you wanted to see yourself as strong - as able to do all that if you wanted to?"

Richard: "I suppose so."

Counsellor: "It is possible, you know, to be strong in different ways. It doesn't have to be physical strength. It can be strength to be brave enough to talk to other people about what is happening for you."

Richard: "Yes, I suppose I try to hide how upset I am from my wife. I don't want to add to her worries. I've brought enough worries to her and the boys."

Counsellor: "Why don't you try sharing some of your fears with her and see how she reacts?"

Richard: "It just seems to be the right thing to do - to keep them to myself. She might think I'm a coward."

Counsellor: "Only a fool would not be afraid just after a heart attack. Anybody would have fears. That's not cowardly. Its just being realistic, isn't it?"

When he was able to develop these new images of himself, Richard's psychological constriction started to loosen and his depression lifted.

CHAPTER 8

IMAGES OF ISOLATION

"You're all on your own with your illness"

(Pat G., heart attack)

People who are ill feel isolated from well people because they believe that their illness-related experiences cannot be understood by them. Images of isolation also develop because people are often physically removed by illness from those who are close to them and because those people withdraw from them. Images of these three kinds will now be explored in this last chapter of Section 2. The first image focusses on lack of understanding. "HEALTHY PEOPLE DON'T UNDERSTAND WHAT IT IS LIKE TO BE ILL". This image of others who are not troubled by illness or injury does not allow them the capacity to empathize with experiences they are not currently having. It draws a line between healthy and ill people over which they cannot step. Like many of the self-defeating images which I selected for discussion in this Section, it is all encompassing in its meaning. "All healthy people are incapable of understanding", it says. People who use such an image also imply that its opposite is true: "Ill people may understand what it is like". This importance of this point becomes clear when it is remembered that such an image is likely to have implications. To use it is to believe: "Healthy people do not understand what it is like to be ill like me". It follows for people who believe this that: "Ill people may understand me". This aspect of this image provides an opportunity for the effective use of the self-help groups which I recommend at the end of this chapter.

The second image of isolation is often expressed in this way. "WHILE I'VE BEEN IN HOSPITAL I HAVE BEEN HOMESICK". It is a less sweeping statement than the first one, that is, it is not an all inclusive image. It refers only to people's experience while hospitalized. Its message, too, is a simpler one. It conveys that the speaker knows that there is a place which is not the hospital and which is much better than the hospital. "Home" has many meanings for different people. I shall speculate on some of them here. It may mean "a familiar place, a place that I know in contrast to the hospital which I do not". It may also mean "a place where I am known", in contrast to the relative anonymity of the hospital. Another interpretation would view "home" as "where my family lives", full of memories of personally significant interactions which are unlikely to occur in a hospital. Yet another views "home" as "a place of safety", a place where the frightening and even painful events which may occur while one is isolated in hospital are unlikely to occur.

"I FIND THAT THE SECRECY OF THE DOCTORS IS HARD TO COPE WITH" is the third image to be explored here. It matters little whether "the doctors" are actually withholding information or are as yet uncertain about the diagnosis. What is important is that the many people who make a statement like this believe them to be keeping secrets about them and their illnesses which they do not know about. They feel, not only isolated, but excluded. Anger often accompanies the construction of this kind of image. The emotion which is explicitly a part of it is helplessness. When these people refer to the secrecy as "hard to cope with", they are saying that they do not know how to deal with it. They would like to do something about it, but they don't know what to do. They believe they lack the ability to change the behaviour of "the doctors" in the way they want. What we know of helplessness-laden images of illness (see Chapter 6) makes clear why.

The discussion of isolation-laden images, the last of the images of illness which are predominantly negative in tone, follows the format of earlier chapters. A sample of such images is described. This includes some which focus on loneliness. Others focus on loss; loss of the understanding and the esteem of others, to name two. Images of isolation accompanied by other images which have already been examined - anger, helplessness and depression - are also explored. Then information about how they occur in reaction to illness and injury, affect recovery and may, of themselves, generate illness is reviewed. At the end of the chapter, I make suggestions about how people can be helped to give up some of their images of isolation.

Some Isolation-Laden Images of Illness

Isolated often implies loneliness. These images have the flavour of loneliness. "THE LONELINESS IS THE WORST THING" is a cry about the "aloneness" of one who is ill. So is "YOU'RE ALL ON YOUR OWN WITH YOUR ILLNESS", which implies that there is no-one with whom to share its burden. Some ill people even feel that there is no-one who is concerned about that burden or about finding ways to deal with it: "THERE DOESN'T SEEM TO BE ANYONE WHO IS INTERESTED IN MY PROBLEM". Often it is because family are unable to maintain contact with them that ill people become lonely: "WHILE I'M IN HOSPITAL, I AM MISSING MY HUSBAND QUITE A BIT. HE CAN'T GET IN HERE MORE THAN ONCE A WEEK". "I'VE GOT NO FAMILY SUPPORT AT THE MOMENT. THEY ARE ALL OVERSEAS". For others, the hospital is full of people who care, while home is the place of isolation and loneliness: "WHEN I GO HOME, IT WILL MEAN BEING ON MY OWN".

Isolation can also mean loss. The experience of social isolation implies losing both the understanding and the esteem of other people. Images involving a lack of understanding by others, one of which has already been noted, have been used by people with a range of health problems. "NO-ONE KNOWS WHAT YOU FEEL LIKE, SITTING IN A WHEELCHAIR". "I'VE HAD NO-ONE TO TALK TO ABOUT THE CANCER - NO DOCTOR, NO FAMILY". "I CAN'T COMMUNICATE WITH MY HUSBAND ABOUT MY DIABETES". "DON'T DEPEND ON YOUR FAMILY. I'VE LEARNED THAT FROM MY HEART ATTACK". Such images can also arise through hospital ward placements which may not be the best for the person who is ill, like this nineteen year-old "surfie" who was placed in a ward of grandfathers: "THERE'S NO-ONE HERE OF MY AGE THAT I CAN TALK TO". This isolation is not so difficult to deal with as that which people believe occurs because of losing the esteem of others through illness-related disability. Two examples, one from a man with AIDS and the other from a woman who was paraplegic, follow. "AIDS HAD MADE ME AN OUTCAST FROM SOCIETY". It is the implications of the image used by the ill person which continues to concern us here, not whether it is accurate or not. "PEOPLE STARE AT YOU WHEN YOU'RE IN A WHEELCHAIR. I DON'T LIKE IT; SO I DON'T GO OUT".

Losses of other kinds can be perceived by ill people to have occurred. For people on special diets it can be the foods they used to enjoy: "I'M PRETTY RESTRICTED IN WHAT I CAN EAT NOW. NO MORE OF THOSE SUGARY CAKES I LIKE TOO MUCH". For people in business on their own, who have been unexpectedly hospitalized, it can be money that they lose: "I'VE LOST A FEW DOLLARS FOR MY TRUCKING BUSINESS THROUGH THIS ACCIDENT". For a family man it can be the ordinary give and take of family life: "WHILE I'M IN HOSPITAL I'LL MISS OUT ON TAKING MY DAUGHTERS TO THEIR SWIMMING LESSONS". Others, in financial difficulties, caused by their illness, may be losing help with their domestic chores: "I'LL HAVE TO GIVE UP MY HOME HELP". Yet others find themselves to be losing people close to them: "MY HUSBAND COULDN'T HANDLE MY ILLNESS, SO HE LEFT ME".

The images of isolation which the ill and injured people of our research project have shared with us are often associated with other strong feelings. Anger is one of these. One such image holds that if people express much anger, they will become isolated: "NOBODY WANTS YOU IF YOU ARE GOING TO BE GRIZZLING ALL THE TIME". Another centres on the anger of the speaker, an epileptic, who seethed at the way he saw himself and his friends in a self-help group for epileptics were treated when they applied for jobs: "WE ARE DISCRIMINATED AGAINST BY THIS LOUSY SOCIETY". A third isolation-laden image associated with anger came from a socially prominant woman who had recovered most of her functioning after a stroke: "I AM AN OUTCAST NOW AT MY BOWLING CLUB". To feel oneself isolated by others often leads to anger.

It can also encourage ill people to generate more images of helplessness. They do not see themselves as controlling their world but it as controlling them. Their bodies are out of control: "I HAVE BEEN LOSING A LOT OF BLOOD". They lack the resources to do what they want to do: "I CAN'T AFFORD TO USE A NEW SYRINGE EVERY TIME I INJECT". They are not able to cope with their isolation-laden images: "ONE OF THE FEELINGS I FOUND HARDEST TO COPE WITH WHEN I WAS ILL WAS...NOBODY UNDERSTOOD". They feel unable to break free of their physical, and for that matter psychological, surroundings to seek contact with others: "I'VE BEEN LIKE A PRISONER LIVING IN SOLITARY CONFINEMENT". People recognizing that their illness is chronic or even progressive may have to admit that they will have to give up their plans for overcoming their isolation and loneliness: "THE SCLEROSIS HAS MEANT GIVING UP MY DREAMS OF MARRIAGE AND A FAMILY".

Isolation-laden images are also associated with depression-laden images. "BEING ALONE LIKE THIS REALLY GETS TO YOU". "IF I'M NOT LOVED BY SOMEONE, I'M NOBODY".

Deprivation of social supports is a common theme for both types of images. "IT'S BEING AMONG PEOPLE THAT I MISS MORE THAN ANYTHING". "I CAN'T BEAR TO THINK WHAT LIFE WOULD BE LIKE WITHOUT THE CHILDREN". "I DON'T SEE MUCH OF MY FAMILY NOW". Sometimes such deprivation is dimly recognized as a factor relevant to the illness: "THE PAIN DIDN'T START UNTIL AFTER THE DIVORCE... I SUPPOSE I MIGHT HAVE BEEN HAVING A REACTION TO IT". Death is also a theme which is common to isolation and depression. Sometimes it is the death of a loved one which leads to loneliness: "I LOST BOTH MY PARENTS DURING THE LAST TWO YEARS. I MISS THEM VERY MUCH". At others it is one's own death which is associated with isolation: "WHEN I'M ALONE AT HOME, I COULD EASILY COLLAPSE AND DIE".

Rather than provide an illustration of the various facets of an image of isolation through comments from a group of people with a particular illness, I want to do so by describing one experience which many hospitalized people have shared. This experience is that of unexpectedly having no visitors at the scheduled visiting hour. There is a deprivation facet to this experience: "NO-ONE HAS COME TO SEE ME. EVERYONE ELSE HAS VISITORS, BUT I HAVE NONE". There is helplessness: "I CAN'T PHONE ANYBODY NOW. IT'S TOO LATE". There is anger too: "GEORGE AND JENNIE MIGHT AT LEAST HAVE COME. THEY LIVE NEAR HERE. I BET THEY'RE SITTING IN FRONT OF THEIR TV SET". Feelings of deprivation are also likely: "ALL THE OTHER PATIENTS ARE ENJOYING THEMSELVES AND I

MISSED OUT". People perceive themselves as low in others' esteem: "NOBODY THOUGHT ENOUGH OF ME TO COME". They see others as incapable of understanding them and their needs: "DIDN'T THEY REALISE THAT I'D WANT TO SEE A FRIENDLY FACE OR TWO?". And their loneliness is paramount: "EVERYONE HAS SOMEBODY WHO HAS COME TO SEE THEM... AND I'M ALL ALONE".

The Implications of Isolation-Laden Images

It is not only our informants who report using many isolation-laden images when they are ill or injured. The research which has been described in the literature supports their claims. People experience illness and injury alone (Van den Berg, 1980). This is especially true if the illness or injury is one which changes one's appearance or one's ways of relating to others. It is true, for example, of severe burns (Andreasen and Norris, 1972), multiple sclerosis (Seidler, 1985), cancer (Bloom and Spiegel, 1984) and AIDS (Feldman and Johnston, 1986; Wolcott et al., 1986). Such changes make it difficult for others, who are hanging on to their old images of the injured person, to respond to him or her. That ill or injured people feel rejected under such circumstances is hardly surprising (Straus, 1975). They sometimes are themselves the ones to withdraw in the face of these difficulties (Worden and Sobel, 1978). If illness can be lonely, so can death (de Beavoir, 1973).

People who come to hospital for treatment are often subjected, unfortunately, to a series of experiences which increases their sense of isolation (Volicer, 1978). As has been noted, the atmosphere of a hospital from the perspective of a "patient" is a highly impersonal one (Anderson, 1981; Taylor, 1979). Some of its routine procedures, too, are designed, so it seems, to isolate people from other people. In the intensive care unit (Hackett, Cassem and Wishnie, 1968) this isolation is for the purpose of careful and continuous observation. In the case of a bone marrow transplant (Wellisch, Fawzey and Yager, 1978) it is in order to protect people from infection. In both cases isolation images are stimulated, as they are by the distance health care professionals sometimes maintain from their "patients" in order to protect themselves (Hinton, 1980). While in hospital, ill people also have to learn to relate to a new set of people around them - the health care professionals (Alonzo, 1984; Cohen and Lazarus, 1979). Learning to satisfy one's interpersonal needs through a group of strangers, especially when one is feeling ill and debilitated, is no easy task (Viney, 1983b).

It becomes a very necessary task because the most important isolation brought about by hospitalization is isolation from family and friends (Ben-Sira, 1984; Rolland, 1987). It dislocates people from their established social network (Lewis and Bloom, 1978-79; Miller, 1978). It can lead, also, to a further reaching disconnectedness from other people (Cassell, 1976a). In a study of people who had been hospitalized with a variety of problems, after only a few days some disturbance in their relationships with family or friends was observed for over a quarter of them (Plutchik et al., 1979). Such disturbance was also found in couples, one of whom was waiting for cardiac surgery

(Radley and Green, 1986). The most unfortunate aspect of this dislocation is that it occurs at a time when people need to have their sources of social support available to them (Viney, 1980). Illness and injury result, for most people, in a period of crisis which is likely to be more quickly and effectively resolved if social supports are available (Viney, 1976). Ill people need to have people about them on whom they can rely (Mechanic, 1977; Wortman and Dunkel-Schetter, 1979). It seems, too, that this need increases with the severity of the illness (Thomas and Weiner, 1974).

If their illness is short-lived, people probably can cope with a brief period of isolation. It is when the illness or the effects of the injury linger that people have to work very hard to maintain the relationships that are important to them (Cohen and Lazarus, 1979). Yet with chronic illness, family and old friends may not be enough. They are not suffering the same disabilities and handicaps as the ill person, nor the pain. They do not, as we have been told, understand. There is a need then, for contact with a group of people like oneself, a group of peers dealing with the same problems and having the same goals. Handicap and disability force new roles on people. They need opportunities to observe others in these roles and to receive empathic support from others while they are trying them for themselves (Adams and Lindemann, 1974; Dean, 1986). They need self-help groups, like those provided successfully for people with cancer (Spiegel, Bloom and Yalom, 1981; Vachon et al., 1982) and rheumatoid and osteo-arthritis (Shearn and Fireman, 1985; Weinberger, Hiner and

Tierney, 1986).

Why are such opportunities so important for ill people? One of their major tasks is to maintain their self-esteem in the face of many unpleasant and demeaning experiences (Cassell, 1976a; Moos and Tsu, 1977). For people functioning well in the wider community, a sense of competence or self-esteem has the same central importance. If people are attractive to others, they relate more to others, develop and practice their interpersonal skills more and come to possess more self-esteem. However, if they are not so attractive to others, they relate less to others, have fewer opportunities to practice their interpersonal skills and their self-esteem falls or remains low (Glidewell, 1972). The same pattern of events can occur for people who are ill. If they lack social support, their distress increases and their self-esteem falls (Silver and Wortman, 1980). Maintaining the self-esteem of ill or injured people is crucial because of the power of self-fulfilling prophecy. People who believe certain things about themselves and others find that events turn out the way they expect (Rosenthal, 1976). People who expect certain things of their illness will see them confirmed (Simonton, Matthews-Simonton and Creighton, 1978). People with high self-esteem have more positive expectations than those whose self-esteem is low, so that ill people's self-esteem should be increased when possible.

This is one explanation of why people who have good social support, when they get ill, have less severe symptoms (Luborsky, Todd and Katcher, 1973). It could also be why people with social support cope better with illness when it comes (Linn and Husaini, 1985; Smith et al., 1985). A similar finding has been observed for the cause and effects of illness. Isolation-laden images, together with fears of body damage, seem to be a good predictor of poor rehabilitation (Viney and Westbrook, 1983c). It is for these reasons that experts have urged that evaluations of rehabilitation programmes should include, among their outcome measures, the development and maintenance of relationships with others (Shontz, 1975; Albrecht and Higgins, 1977). There is also some evidence available that people who maintain satisfying relationships are less prone to illness and injury (Kaplan, Cassell and Gore, 1977; Lynch, 1977).

Coping with Images of Isolation

We have seen that the images of isolation used by people who are ill focus on loss as well as loneliness, especially loss of understanding and esteem from others. We have also seen how isolation-laden images may be associated with some of the negatively toned images which have been discussed earlier, especially images of anger, helplessness and depression. The experiences of hospitalized people who unexpectedly have no visitors at visiting time makes clear how these images flood into one's mind. How illness and its attendant treatments can generate isolation-laden images has been explored, as has the effects on self-esteem of a sense of isolation. The likelihood that these images are associated with more severe symptoms of illness, with poor handling of them and even with the initial development of such illness makes it appropriate to examine ways of breaking up images of isolation and substituting more positive ones. This can be done through direct invalidation of such images by a counsellor, accompanied by validation of new images (Epting, 1984). It can be done by encouraging family or friends to accomplish the same ends, as a counsellor's interaction with a man who has been admitted for a genital operation and his family shows. It can also be achieved through work with groups of other ill people, especially in self-help groups of people with similar health problems. In this work it is important to establish whether the ill people have isolated themselves, or whether isolation is thrust upon them by their illness-related circumstances. If the former, the cause is likely to be their images of illness which need to be explored further. If the latter, other techniques, such as those reported here, may be useful.

Images of isolation are one kind of image which it is difficult to deal with alone. It is hard to change your image of others as ignoring or rejecting one without new input from them. Of course people who feel isolated may find it hard to trust others too. For this reason, one of the most effective ways to learn to deal with these images is with a professional counsellor who helps the ill person test his or her isolation-laden images and find them wanting (Viney, 1981a). An example might be the one cited at the beginning of this chapter: "HEALTHY PEOPLE DO NOT KNOW WHAT IT IS LIKE TO BE ILL". As a physiotherapist empathized with her feelings, the woman who believed this to be true soon discoverd that it is not true for all people who are healthy, that is, not for the physiotherapist and perhaps not for some nurses or physicians. She also learned, when she tested it with some of her fellow "patients" that its reverse is not necessarily true either. Because people become ill like oneself, that does not make them immediately able to understand one's feelings or take on one's perspective. After many more experiments with the counsellor and with other people she discarded her old image in favour of one which would work better for her. It was something like this: "SOME PEOPLE WILL UNDERSTAND WHAT IT IS LIKE FOR ME TO BE ILL, IF I TELL THEM HONESTLY AND THEY LISTEN TO ME CAREFULLY".

Sometimes a change like this can best be triggered by someone who works with both the person who is ill and his or her family in a counselling role (Proctor, 1985). Gordon M. illustrates the success of this approach. He was admitted to hospital for surgical exploration of a lump on one of his testes. His wife and 14 year old son visited him regularly before and after his operation; but his 16 year old daughter, whose photograph he showed with pride to the staff, did not visit him. While waiting for the results of this exploration, he was able to talk to his physician.

Gordon: "I am feeling pretty tense. I suppose my daughter doesn't want to see her old dad in the hospital".

Physician: "Can you understand why she might not want to come?"

Gordon: "Well... I suppose she just doesn't care about the operation. None of the family thinks it is at all serious".

Physician: "What about you? Do you consider it to be serious?"

Gordon: "I do. I mean, it could be cancer couldn't it? The way they go on, you'd think I was having a toenail trimmed".

Physician: "You feel as if they don't care about you much, as you sit here worrying about it all".

Gordon: "It does hurt a bit... I do miss my daughter".

After helping Gordon identify and express some of his isolation-laden images, the physician arranged to meet with his wife when she came to visit him. She explained that his daughter was not visiting him because she was so worried about him that the family were afraid that she would let him know this and upset him further. A dominant image for the family turned out to be: "DON'T SHOW YOUR FEELINGS TOO MUCH OR YOU'LL BE SORRY".

Gordon's wife: "But we've always said about worries that it doesn't do to play them up".

Physician: "And if this makes it difficult to know when to show concern for your family...?"

Gordon's wife: "Oh, it doesn't. Anyway, sometimes sympathy can just make things worse".

Physician: "Mrs. M., when people are in hospital and away from their families they sometimes find it hard to remember that they care about them. And when they are worried about something and they have no-one to talk to about it, that worry grows".

Gordon's wife: "I don't want that to happen to Gordon. I hadn't realized... What do you think I should say to him?"

Physician: "You could ask him about the operation and how he feels about it, not sympathising, just listening. Of course he might get upset; but that would be better than his bottling up those feelings inside. Not talking about his fears will not make them go away".

Gordon's wife: "Do you think Julie might come to see him?"

Physician: "I'm sure he'd be pleased if she did - especially if she shares her feelings with him".

The physician was not trying to bring about a major change in the images held in common by Gordon's family, but to effect a minor change so that his wife could be more supportive of him during his period of crisis.

Family and friends who come to visit ill people are, however, often aware of the images of isolation which seem to swamp them but are not sure how to deal with them. Van den Berg (1980) has used his understanding of ill people's images to make some useful suggestions for their visitors. He advocates treating them as usual but remembering the differences between the images of people confined to bed and the images of their active and mobile visitors. He advises letting ill people take the lead and giving them time, one of our most precious commodities. Talking does not always imply meaningful communication. This is often best maintained with ill people, whose energy is depleted, through non-verbal means such as eye contact, smiling and touching and even through companionable silences. Often ill people's images of isolation can be broken down by the sharing of a simple pleasure with a visitor, for example, a game or a joke.

Our examination of images of isolation constructed by people who are ill has suggested that they may best be broken down through people's participation in self-help groups. These groups are often set up for people with specific health problems, for example, for leukaemics, or people with multiple sclerosis or people who know that they have tested HIV antibody positive or developed AIDS. Many of them are run by professional health care givers (Blumberg, Flaherty and Lewis, 1980; Grant and Anns, 1988; Mitchell and Glicksman, 1977; Wellisch, 1981). For people who are ill, exchanging experiences with other people with similar problems provides invalidation of isolation-laden images: "There are other people like me". It gives a sense of solidarity as common goals are pursued. Support is also available and valuable feedback about oneself and one's images can be had for the asking. A variety of possible solutions to common problems are demonstrated by other group members and so can be evaluated: "I DON'T KNOW HOW TO HANDLE MY INCREASING DEPENDENCY ON PEOPLE. I DON'T LIKE THE WAY JIM IS REVELLING IN IT. BUT BILL, HE SEEMS TO HANDLE IT WELL. HOW DOES HE DO IT?" In this atmosphere, it is possible to express one's feelings freely and to be understood by others. There are opportunities, too, for empathic listening to others and for increased self-esteem because of what one proves able to offer to the rest of the group.

Groups which do not contain any health care professionals can also be useful in breaking down images of isolation. They are usually more informal and less inclined to be judgmental, and so give ill people more opportunity for spontaneous self-expression (Gartner and Riessman, 1977). Because they are made up of "insiders", a warm, supportive atmosphere is quickly achieved (Hurvitz, 1974). There can be no elitism in these groups. Nor is there any mystification that might be, albeit inadvertently, introduced by professionals. Whatever is accomplished by the group, the group members come to recognize that they are doing it for themselves (Blumberg, Flaherty and Lewis, 1980). Their self-esteem can be considerably raised by this knowledge, as well as by the support they receive. All members can come to identify in themselves capacities for problem solving and growth. These capacities are recognized as their own rather than those of "the experts".

SECTION 3

MORE WELCOME IMAGES OF ILLNESS

Not all the images of illness developed in our culture are distressing in their effects. While anxiety-laden and depression-laden images, for example, seem to be common, so are images containing good feelings. Severe illness and injury can be viewed with humour and even happiness. It can also be interpreted in terms of, not helplessness, but competence and control. It can lead, not to images of isolation, but to images of support and friendship. I deal with these three types of more welcome images in Section 3. I have organized each chapter in a format similar to that of Section 2. Expressions of these images by the participants in our research programme are considered first; then some of their implications are examined. The last section of each chapter deals with how these more facilitating and helpful, as well as more enjoyable, images can be developed and elaborated by people who are ill, and how they can be encouraged in this task by health care professionals.

CHAPTER 9

HAPPY IMAGES AND HUMOUR

"I have everything to live for!"

(Jenny D., cancer)

We have known for some time that even the most disruptive of crises generates some good feelings (Visotsky et al., 1961). Psychologists have been criticized for not putting as much effort into their investigation of these positive aspects of experience as they have into negative aspects, such as images of anxiety, anger and depression (Maslow, 1956). However, it is becoming clear that people in our culture do not talk as much about positive as negative experiences, nor do they differentiate much between different types of good feeling (Westbrook, 1976). That is why this chapter is about the generally positively toned images of ill people and is followed, in this section, by only two more chapters. They deal with the two main focal points of the positive experiences which the people who spoke with us have described: positive feelings about oneself, expressed in images of competence and control, and positive feelings about one's relationships with others, expressed in images involving family and friends. The development and maintenance of both of these kinds of images are believed to be important for psychological maturity (Greenberger and Sorensen, 1974).

Less specific good feelings are mainly manifested in people's images of happiness. "THE OPERATION, THE PAIN, THE HOSPITALIZATION - IT'S ALL BEEN WORTHWHILE". This is an image which recognizes the difficulties which have arisen. Operations, pain and hospitalization are all distressing and hard to deal with. Yet the person who said this now judges that it has all been transcended by her present happiness. She does not make clear what her specific sources of happiness are. Some of them may be relief that it is all over. Her satisfaction may also have much to do with the effects of the operation on her physical well-being and so on her quality of life. There may even have been other aspects of her surgery-related experience which provided ample compensation for its more negative side, for example, in the way it gave her family an opportunity to express its love for her. She also implies in this image that her suffering might not have been "worthwhile". She might have been left sore and sorry, with nothing much achieved. She is glad that this did not happen.

For those who are chronically ill and so cannot experience the joys of recovery, a more common and yet still positive image is this. "UNTIL YOU ARE ILL, YOU DON'T REALLY APPRECIATE THE GOOD THINGS IN LIFE". This image of illness allows it one compensating feature at least. Illness often makes people aware of themselves and their world in a new way (Van den Berg, 1980). Being threatened with death makes them value life. Facing a long period of life in which its quality may be reduced makes them value the quality that remains. There is quality there. There are "good things" to be "appreciated". This is a change for the better that many ill people experience for themselves. They see it as a change, not in their worlds but in themselves. They begin to look more at themselves, their relationships with others and many other good things which they come to prize. I will examine more examples of this kind of valuing later in this chapter.

Humour, because it is an important way of generating happiness and good feelings, will also be explored here. This humourous image provides the first example. "THE DOCTOR HAS BEEN FEEDING ME SO MANY PILLS THAT WHEN YOU SHAKE ME I RATTLE". The laughter provoked by this metaphorical description of oneself as a pill bottle can be very helpful. This humourous image also allows the speaker to distance himself from some of the illness-related events which are making him anxious and angry: his passivity in accepting "the doctor's" recommendations and his fear that the pills might not be doing him any more good than pills do for a pill bottle. Creating such an image gives him some modicum of the control over the situation which he wants. It may also provide him with an opportunity to free up his view of his treatment; so that he can at least make appropriate enquiries about its effects and the likely effects of alternatives. He may eventually come to participate more in the decisions made about the care of his own body for which, as represented by a plastic pill bottle, he has become an uninvolved recipient.

What follows is an account of some generally positive images. Some of these involve the need of ill people to maintain positive images to compensate for their distress. Others are wide in their focus, while yet others deal with the more specific aspects of illness-related events such as recovery, appreciating what one has and enjoying relationships with others. Some examples of humourous images available to ill people are considered. I have also paid some attention to how the humour is created: by an unexpected twist, reversal, exaggeration or minimization, irony or metaphor. A review of the information which is available to relate images of happiness and humour to illness is provided. It deals first with any relationships between them and the development of illness, then with rehabilitation and recovery. It finally examines the frequency of such image use by ill people. The value of optimistic coping for ill and injured people is also explored. Humour is more clearly defined, so that it can be more readily created. Some of its benefits are discussed. The final concern of this chapter is how happy and humour-laden images can be created and maintained.

Some Happy and Humour-Laden Images

Many ill and injured people recognize that they need to maintain some positive images day by day, so that their negatively-toned images do not overwhelm them. "SINCE I'VE BEEN ILL, I TRY TO MAKE THE BEST OF THINGS" is a statement which describes this determinedly optimistic approach. It implies that people should not let themselves be dominated by their pain or handicaps but focus on the interesting and enjoyable aspects of their lives as well. "YOU MUST THINK POSITIVELY ABOUT SOMETHING LIKE THIS ACCIDENT" is a similar kind of interpretation. Ill and injured people also recognize that they, like other people, need to have some event in the future to which they are looking with pleasurable anticipation. "IT'S A MISTAKE NOT TO HAVE SOMETHING GOOD COMING TO GIVE YOU A BIT OF A

BOOST". Especially if people cannot look forward to recovery they must find other sources of future pleasure to look forward to: a favourite meal, a night out to see a film or the visit of an old friend.

Many generally positive images of happiness are used by ill people. Sometimes they focus on the ill person, himself or herself: "I'VE GOT A PRETTY HAPPY NATURE". Sometimes, they focus on sources of happiness available to oneself but not to others: "I'VE GOT MY FAITH IN GOD TO SEE ME THROUGH". More often, they involve an evaluation of the quality of life that the ill person is experiencing. "THERE ARE A LOT MORE POSITIVES IN MY LIFE THAN NEGATIVES" was the perhaps surprising summation of a thirty-seven year old woman who, having lived alone with multiple sclerosis for several years, had just had to have a mastectomy because of suspected cancer in her breast. Others who are facing death find that: "I HAVE EVERYTHING TO LIVE FOR". And even after being admitted to an intensive care unit because of a heart attack it is possible to create an image of this kind: "I'M FEELING VERY SAFE AND SECURE AT THE MOMENT". This speaker's image was, after all, an accurate one in the sense that that unit is likely to be, given the possible condition of his heart, the safest place for him (Hackett, Cassem and Wishnie, 1968).

Another major focus of positive images is an improvement in physical well-being. Just before surgery it is difficult for people to retain such images, although some do manage to do so: "LAST TIME I HAD THIS OPERATION, I PROFITTED FROM IT A GOOD DEAL". It is easier, even with chronic illness, to develop them when some good rehabilitation is observed. "I'M DOING SO WELL". "I'VE GOT SO MUCH USE OF MY ARM BACK THAT I'M THRILLED". Of course nothing leads to the happiness that total recovery does: "I FEEL ONE HUNDRED PER CENT BETTER IN MYSELF". Regaining one's health is very much appreciated: "IT'S REALLY GOOD TO FEEL HEALTHY". When recovery takes place, health can become people's most important asset: "NOTHING ELSE COUNTS REALLY, BESIDES HEALTH. TO BE HEALTHY IS TO BE HAPPY".

If recovery is not possible, ill people can still enjoy what is available to them. Avoiding death is one source of pleasure: "JUST BEING ALIVE IS GOOD". Discovering that life has much to offer can be pleasurable too. "I'VE REALLY GOT SOMETHING TO LOOK FORWARD TO". So can scoring victories over that enemy, illness: "I'VE GOT ANOTHER WRINKLE; AND THAT SHOWS I'VE LIVED ANOTHER YEAR. THAT'S TERRIFIC". As has been noted already, people who have been touched by death often come to value life more. "I TRY TO LIVE EACH MOMENT OF THE TIME AS IF IT WERE VERY PRECIOUS". "THE SIMPLEST THINGS IN LIFE SEEM LOVELY TO YOU - THE GRASS, THE INSECTS, THE SKY!" Even the illness itself can be seen as having a positive effect, as for this woman dealing with cancer. "THE MASTECTOMY HAS HELPED ME IMPROVE MY LIFE, STRANGELY ENOUGH. I'M NOW PREPARED TO TRY ANYTHING. I'VE EVEN TAKEN UP RIDING". A variety of compensations for the suffering of illness are found, for example, "I WAS VERY LUCKY TO

GET THIS BED WITH A VIEW OF THE OCEAN". The young woman, with cancer as well as multiple sclerosis, who was calculating her balance sheet found this on the credit side: "I DON'T FEAR DEATH; THAT'S A PLUS ON MY PAGE".

Images of enjoyable relationships with other people will be explored more fully in Chapter 11; but because they are the focus of many of the happy images which ill people maintain, I shall give some examples of them here. The family is one source of pleasure. "MY HUSBAND IS VERY GOOD TO ME". "I ENJOY BEING WITH MY WIFE AND CHILDREN". "I'M EXTRA HAPPY TODAY BECAUSE I AM GOING HOME TO THE FAMILY". Another is friends. "THE VISITING HOUR IS THE NICEST PART OF BEING IN HOSPITAL. ALL YOUR FRIENDS COME TO SEE YOU". "BEING ILL DOES MAKE YOU APPRECIATE YOUR REAL FRIENDS". Yet another is the staff of health care professionals who make contact with the ill person. "I ENJOYED THIS STAY IN HOSPITAL, BECAUSE THE STAFF WAS SO GOOD" and "I ALWAYS COME BACK TO THIS HOSPITAL, BECAUSE THE PEOPLE HERE ARE SO NICE". Good feelings are stimulated both by the almost magical feats of the medical practitioners, "DR. _____ DID A WONDERFUL JOB WITH MY LAST OPERATION", and the round-the-clock care and attention of the nurses, "THE NURSES ARE GREAT! THEY ARE SO HELPFUL".

Humour-laden images can be built in a variety of ways. One is by an unexpected but neat twist in a narrative (Viney, 1985a) as in this elderly man's account of the whistle he kept by his wheel chair. "MY

METHOD OF COMMUNICATION IS A DIRTY BIG WHISTLE; AND I GET BOTH MY DOG AND MY DAUGHTER WITH IT AT THE SAME TIME". This is another example from a diabetic. "YOU CAN'T WALK INTO A RESTAURANT AND ASK FOR A DIET PAVLOVA". This image is from a young man frustrated by the length of his stay in hospital. "I'M A BIT FUCKED OFF. EXCUSE MY FRENCH!" He was embarrassed by his swearing and joked by moving his focus from it to the unexpected one of "French", unexpected because the French language is commonally used by well-educated, cultured people and not by people who swear. Exaggeration can be humourous, as this woman reported cheerfully after her mastectomy. "THE SISTER ASKED MY HUSBAND, WHAT ARE YOU GOING TO DO WHEN YOU LOOK AT YOUR WIFE'S SCAR TISSUE? HE JUST LAUGHED AND SAID: I HAVEN'T LOOKED AT HER FOR YEARS!" Minimization, its opposite can be humourous too, as this stroke victim demonstrated. "MY LIFE AT THE MOMENT IS LIKE THE WEATHER - FINE AND MILD". Irony is another form of humour which is often used by people like this man with high blood pressure. "I DRINK SODA WATER NOW, INSTEAD OF BEER... AND I DON'T HAVE TO WORRY ABOUT THE BREATHALISER ON THE WAY HOME".

One of the most common forms of humour used by the people we have interviewed is that of metaphor or simile. This involves the likening of the illness or illness-related events to images of other events which are in part appropriately similar but in part inappropriately different. One emphysema sufferer reported: "I'D

COME HOME FEELING THAT I'D RUN A MARATHON IN THE OLYMPIC GAMES". He was exhausted because of his reduced oxygen supply; but his day had been much slower and less demanding than that of an athlete. This mixing of dissimilar images is also done with humour by a diabetic who likened herself to a horse: "MY FRIENDS SAY, SEE, SHE'S ALWAYS EATING. SHE'S GOT THE CHAFF BAG ON AGAIN". It is the theme of a quadraplegic youth: "I HAVE TO HAVE SOMEONE WITH ME 24 HOURS A DAY. IT'S JUST LIKE HAVING A BABY SITTER". This comparison was a bitter-sweet one, since, while he enjoyed being looked after like a baby, he did not want to be as helpless as a baby. Perhaps the most vivid and yet gently humourous image of physical deterioration was shared with us by a ninety-year old man who was experiencing failure in the functioning of many of his body organs. "HERE AT THE HOSPITAL YOU OUGHT TO HAVE A SCRAP YARD FOR BODIES LIKE THEY HAVE FOR OLD CARS. YOU COULD DO AWAY WITH THE OLD JUNK AND KEEP THE SPARE PARTS. THEY MIGHT BE GOOD FOR SOMEONE ELSE". He had signed a donor-form for his still fully-functioning kidneys.

Humour does not seem to be used by one group of ill people more than any others. Let us look, however, at the kinds of humourous observations diabetics make, as one example. They express some generally positively toned images, such as: "I'VE GOT SUCH A LOT GOING FOR ME. I COUNT MY BLESSINGS". They learn to appreciate those parts of their lives which are not in the shadow cast by their illness: "WHEN YOU'VE GOT THE PROPER AMOUNT OF INSULIN INSIDE YOU, YOU'RE AS WELL AS ANYBODY". They also appreciate the people around them: "I'VE GOT A GOOD WIFE". They can joke about the dietary restrictions placed on them: "I HAVE BEEN CONDEMNED TO SALADS FOR THE REST OF MY NATURAL LIFE". No doubt this image of sentencing to an indefinite term of imprisonment seems an appropriate one at times. Diabetics can even joke about the paradoxical nature of the demands their illness places on them. "PROVIDED THAT YOU REMEMBER TWENTY-FOUR HOURS PER DAY THAT YOU ARE A DIABETIC, THEN YOU CAN FORGET ABOUT BEING A DIABETIC".

The Implications of Happy Images and Humour

The relationship between images containing these positive feelings and recovery from illness is a complex one. On the one hand, people recovering from surgery have been found to do so more quickly if their morale is high (Brown and Rawlinson, 1976). Raising of morale is seen as important to cancer sufferers too (Noyes, 1981; Roud, 1986-87); indeed they have been encouraged to create positive images of their body overcoming their illness (Simonton, Matthews-Simonton and Creighton, 1978). The ability to balance some of one's negative images by positive ones has also been linked with good coping with illness (Blumberg, Flaherty and Lewis, 1980; Worden and Sobel, 1978). On the other hand, it seems that positively toned images which embody an acceptance of the illness (Derogatis,

Abeloff and Melisaratos, 1979) or the sick role associated with it (Byrne, White and Butler, 1981) can lead to the acceptance of death which is usually a sign that life will end soon (Kubler-Ross, 1969). Happy images, then, may aid recovery; but contented acceptance of the illness and illness-related events may be a prelude to death.

It may even be that to be happier is to be less vulnerable to illness (Antonovsky, 1980). If this is so, how does this link between physical and psychological events occur? At this time the answer appears to be that stress leads to illness through at least two physiological mechanisms: our physiological homeostasis and the effectiveness of our immune systems (Gottschalk, 1985). The functioning of our immune systems, which is only recently being explored, appears to be adversely affected by negative psychological states brought about by stress (Udelman and Udelman, 1983). Bereavement with its anxiety, depression and anger has also been linked with abnormal immune function (Bartop, Lazarus and Luckhurst et al., 1977; Irwin, Daniels and Weiner, 1987; Schleifer, Keller and Mamerino et al., 1983). Positive states such as happiness and hope, then, may be associated with more effective functioning of our immune systems.

Given the negatively toned images of uncertainty, anxiety, helplessness, anger, depression and loneliness we have seen ill people use (see Section 2), it does not seem likely that they would use many positively toned images. In fact, they do. Optimism is a common reaction to illness, even chronic illness like asthma (Kinsman et al.,

1976). Chronically ill people dealing with a range of health problems have been shown to express more positive feeling (Viney and Westbrook, 1986) and to prefer more optimistic coping than people who are not ill (Viney and Westbrook, 1984). While they may not be able to enjoy sexual activities to the full, they do enjoy exchanges of affection with their partners (Lieber et al., 1976). The more severe the illness, the stronger the expression of positive feelings (Hamera and Shontz, 1978). Such happy images are associated with fewer anxiety-laden images (see Chapter 4) and more images of competence (see Chapter 10). People with heart conditions seem to prefer more optimistic coping than people with other chronic conditions (Viney and Westbrook, 1984). The less severe both the observed disability and the handicap people perceive themselves to have, the more positive feeling they express (Viney and Westbrook, 1981a; 1984). Positively-toned images are also more common, not so surprisingly, for people who are experiencing good rehabilitation (Viney and Westbrook, 1982c).

But are these positively-toned images produced by people who are ill genuine expressions of enjoyment for their own sake or evidence of avoidance or denial of their more negative feelings? In other words, do they represent flexible, reality-oriented coping or of rigid, reality-distorting defensiveness? A study comparing ill people with different levels of positive feeling on their other emotional states was carried out to answer that question. It showed that much positive feeling was associated with evidence of flexible coping, indicating that genuine enjoyment does occur (Viney, 1986). A more recent study with people who have tested as HIV antibody positive also supported this view, although not so strongly (Viney, et al., 1987).

Active coping with illness or injury, when compared with merely accepting what that illness or injury brings, can be seen to be an essentially optimistic activity (Weisman and Sobel, 1979). It is concerned with setting goals for the future with the positive expectation that at least some of them will be achieved. Hope is the positive emotion which is involved here. It is ironic that so little has been written about the role of hope in illness and recovery (Menninger, 1959; Gottschalk and Gleser, 1969; Stotland, 1969; Shontz, 1977), when, as we have seen, ill people are often aware of the importance to them of maintaining some positive expectations of the future. Every health care professional, who knows how these expectations work to make even placebo treatments effective, knows the importance of hope too (Hutschnecker, 1981). It, like other more welcome images, can be hard to sustain in the face of prolonged and severe illness. One of the best ways to create and maintain hopeful and positive images is humour. Laughter may be, as the Readers ' Digest has described it, the best medicine.

Of the many accounts of the healing powers of laughter, the best known is probably that about Norman Cousins (1979), the editor of the Saturday Review. He suffered a severe illness which was considered by his medical practitioners to be life-threatening. Having worked so much with humour, he set about treating himself with it. He laughed his way through many Marx brothers films and Candid Camera reruns until he regained his health. That Cousins is not the only one to have faith in the power of laughter is witnessed by the very large number of jokes about hospitals, nurses and medical practitioners which are to be found. As Max Beerbohm pointed out, of all our forefathers who have died before us, none has been known to die of laughter. Yet jokes are not always humourous. A joke told to someone else can fall flat if it is not presented in a way that is meaningful to him or her. Joking to an ill person or about illness can also fall flat if it is done without understanding and gentleness. It can become an alien intrusion. Humour, because it is better integrated into ongoing interactions between people, is rarely so alien. Let me explain what I mean by humour.

Humour is a creative act, very much like the act of image building (Koestler, 1964). It involves juggling with multiple meanings (O'Connell, 1981) and reversals of these meanings or images, as has been noted earlier. Using humour to deal with a problem consists of using two sets of images of it at once as in a metaphor (Gordon, 1978). Humour accepts images which are common or shared by people but deals with others in fantasy (Sveback, 1974). The effect of this occurring unexpectedly is to shake up both sets of images of the problem and so make them more flexible and open to change (Jasnow, 1981). This provides the opportunity for a temporary side step away from what is assumed to be "reality" to other images of events, these images also being shared with others (Viney, 1985a).

Laughter results. These aspects of humour can be seen in the humour of the elderly man who proposed that hospitals have a junk yard for human parts. He built up two sets of images, one of human bodies which are no longer useful, the other of no longer useful machines. Both sets of images were shared by him with others. This examination of illness-related events freed up his images enough so that he came to see that there were some part of his old body which might be useful to others, and maybe even some parts of himself. Given this definition of humour, a sense of humour is considered to be the capacity to accept and deal with other people's images without destroying one's own (Sveback, 1974).

What purposes can ill people's use of humour serve? Defining humour in this way makes clear how it can cut into the inflexibility which can be built into the images of ill people through their uncertainty, anxiety and depression (Carter and Orfandis, 1976; Jasnow, 1981). It leads to a wider range of choices among the images people use to make sense of illness-related events. It also lends a distance from and so perspective on those events (Farrelly and Brandsma, 1974; O'Connell, 1981). Often this new perspective leads to new images, giving ill people a kind of power over their world (Levine, 1977). Humour is particularly effective in breaking up some of the negatively toned images with which we have dealt. It can reduce anxiety-laden images (Carter and Orfandis, 1976; Kuhlman, 1984), especially those which are ridden with embarrassment (Viney, 1979). It permits expression of anger-laden images, but in a socially acceptable way (Viney, 1985a). Perhaps the most important function of humour is to maintain positive images of oneself as one interacts with others. It involves a sharing of images and laughter which creates bonds between people (Gruner, 1978; Kane, Suls and Tedeschi, 1977; Narboe, 1981). It can also be used to loosen those bonds, that is, to indicate gently that one no longer subscribes to the goals and values of a particular group (Viney, 1985a).

I know of only one report on the humour created by ill people in hospitals (Coser, 1959). Its writer was impressed by their use of it to create bonds between them. Through it, she saw that they communicate information to one another, and even reassurance. Information about threatening medical procedures can be conveyed to enable others to prepare more effectively for them. They can also be made less threatening by joking about them. She also noted that hospitalized people use humour to help one another create new images of themselves and illness-related events. "Patients", as we have seen, have little prestige in the hospital setting, so that they often feel insecure and helpless. Sharing jokes about the health care professionals helps to raise themselves to their level and, at the same time, contributes to the development of a warm relationship among the participants. Humour, then, can be a powerful tool for people who are ill, although it must be used with sensitivity by both professionals and family members (Saper, 1987).

Developing Happy Images and Humour

This chapter has been dealing with images of illness and injury which are generally positive. In it, we have explored the need for such images which ill people recognize in themselves, the images which determinedly focus on their blessings and those which stem more spontaneously from their recovery. We have seen that, even when total recovery is not possible, people build positively toned images around appreciating what they have, especially their relationships with others. Since humour is one of the best ways of developing positive images, some humour from ill people has been examined. Examples of all these interpretations of illness-related events have been given by diabetics. Information about the important part positive images play in recovery has been provided, together with a reminder that positive images which consist merely of acceptance of illness or the sick role can be the forerunner of acceptance of death. Positive images which contain a picture of life as a challenge are more likely to precede recovery: images of hope, for example. Humour can help to free up old images and develop new ones. It can also aid ill people in many other ways. How ill people can increase their use of humour is therefore explored, together with an approach based on humour which can be employed by counsellors working with them. As in other chapters, a concluding interaction between an ill person and a counsellor is included to illustrate several of these points.

When we tease someone, it is a way of saying to them: "Your view of the world is not the only one. Your images can do with a shaking up" (Mancuso, 1979). If I think, for example, that the image a friend has of himself has become unrealistically good and that he is boasting inappropriately, I may tease him by saying: "When is that balloon of yours going to burst". I convey to him, gently because it is with humour, that I think his self-image has become overinflated. In other words, humour can be used to comment on images. Ill people can do this for themselves. It can be done in the hospital bed and without the knowing participation of other people. A young man, after a motor cycle accident, had an arm and two legs in traction for several months. He developed a humourous alter ego in the form of a bear who, unlike him, could go everywhere and do every thing he wanted (like kissing pretty nurses) because he was invisible. This imagined creature enabled this injured man to express many feelings he could not otherwise express, gave him some control over his world and provided him, through its humour, with a commentary on some of his illness-related images.

Although sharing humour has many advantages, humour can be effective, as this example shows, when one is alone. A sense of humour is an invaluable asset for ill people. To develop such a sense is the goal of natural high therapy, a technique designed to help people experience enjoyment and happiness without the aid of unnatural substances, such as alcohol or other drugs, in their bodies (O'Connell, 1981). It recognizes two bases of humour as especially important. These are the self-esteem and interpersonal concern of the humourist. Without these characteristics the humourist cannot move flexibly from one frame of reference to another, from one image to another (O'Connell, 1975). Such humour also permits acceptance of some of the existential paradoxes of humanity: that we can be both sad and glad, for example, or that we can be both gods and mortals. Both of these paradoxes are apparent every day to people who are severely ill. Recognition of them loosens the hold of some of their more dominant and less flexible images.

While humour can be used when alone, it can also be used effectively by a counsellor who wants his or her clients to learn their own self worth, to assert themselves appropriately and to take risks when necessary. It can be used a little by family and friends, too, so long as it is with care and concern. One way counsellors do this is to "provoke" clients. This is done gently, using images that make sense to the clients, and with humour (Farrelly and Brandsma, 1974). Humour is considered to be essential. If clients do not laugh at the counsellor's "provocation", that provocation could prove to be destructive. The counselling process itself becomes like children's play but, like that play, it contains a commentary on the interactions that are taking place and the images inherent in them. Humour can be developed as we have seen, through unexpected but neat accounts of events, reversals, exaggerations or minimizations, irony and metaphors. It can also develop through the less gentle techniques of sarcasm, ridicule and mimicry. Humourous images of oneself, developed in these ways, indicate a flexibility in one's approach to life. Freud (1928) viewed humour as an effective means for coping with stress. He did not view it as a good way of adjusting to life in general. Nowadays, however, humourous images of oneself are recognized as a sign of psychological maturity (Farrelly and Brandsma, 1974; O'Connell, 1981).

Happiness accompanies those sets of images which have been frequently confirmed as providing good ways of anticipating events (McCoy, 1980). Negative feelings flow from images which permit only poor prediction of the future; positive feelings flow from those which provide good prediction. Humour contributes to happiness because it provides a commentary on the relationship of one's images to what is assumed by others to be reality. It recognizes each person's role in building these images and the chasm that can yawn between them and that reality. The following interaction with a young paraplegic, Andy S., shows these recognitions as they develop. The counsellor spoke with him initially some six months after his accident, because he was considered to be uncooperative in his rehabilitation programme.

Counsellor: "Andy, how are things with you?"

Andy (clenching and unclenching his hands): "I am pissed off! I've been in this wheelchair for four months now; and I'm sick of it. I've had no movement in my legs at all. I know they can move. They should have moved by now".

Counsellor: "What have the medical staff said to you about this, Andy?"

Andy: "Nothing much! They just mumble a lot, and hum and haw..."

The counsellor was somewhat surprised by this comment, since the medical staff had made several determined efforts to convey to Andy that he was unlikely to walk again.

On the next few occasions that she met with Andy, the counsellor found him depressed and anxious. He was expressing less frustration, but he was also less alert and interested in his world. He was able, however, to come to trust her. Gently, and on the basis of this trust, she used irony to focus on the gap between his image of his future mobility and that of the professionals. He reacted at first with anger but was later able to accept her message.

Andy: "You are right, you know. It's as if I've been wearing earplugs or filters or something like that. I sort of knew what the doctors were saying; but I didn't let myself hear it".

When his image of his future mobility altered to one which gave him better predictions of his capacity, his anxiety and depression decreased markedly. He even started to create a little humour of his own.

Andy: "You should have seen me this morning at Physiotherapy. They let me slip out of my chair as they were transferring me. There I was on the floor, as flat as a flounder!"

With this humour he was exploring and gaining a perspective on many aspects of his new role as a paraplegic that were distressing to him, for example, his dependence on others, his lack of control and his embarrassment about how he might appear to others. With more effective images he also expressed more positive feelings.

Andy: "I don't like not being able to walk; but I'm coming to terms with it. And there are many things I can still do that I get a kick out of".

Counsellor: "Even though you're in a wheelchair, you can still enjoy yourself. (Pause). Not walking has worried you though. Have you been worried about any other possible results of you accident?"

Andy: "To tell the truth......I was a bit worried about the Old Bill. If I couldn't get my penis up that was going to take some fun out of things. But there is movement in it and the doctors say it will be OK. I'm pretty pleased about that."

CHAPTER 10

IMAGES OF COMPETENCE

"My philosophy of life is that nothing's impossible".

(Susan T., stroke)

"I TRY TO KEEP MYSELF ALERT AND INTERESTED IN THE WORLD OUTSIDE". This is the kind of image of competence and self-control which seems to be hard for ill people to retain. They can be compared with the images of helplessness (which were explored in Chapter 6) which seem to flourish in the hospital milieu. Effort is a key concept in images of this kind (Westbrook and Viney, 1980). Their creator is aware of striving to accomplish something which may not come easily. It is true that it is difficult for someone who is ill, and whose energy is consequently depleted, to make an effort. It is also true, for this particular image, that bed-ridden people find it difficult to reach beyond their physically limited world. That is no reason, however, why ill people cannot conceive of themselves as making an effort. Effort is always relative to ability. It remains effort whether it results in the twitching of a hitherto immobile finger or the Herculean achievement of cleaning the Aegian stables.

Images of competence are not often found together with the negative images which have been explored in Section 2. They are more often constructed at the same time as images which involve good feelings (Viney, 1981b). The reason for this can be seen in another image of competence which contrasts with the first. "I'M NOT THE KIND OF PERSON WHO GIVES IN TO ILLNESS" is a self-description which indicates a belief in one's own ability to survive stress, even the stress of illness. It implies that there are people who let illness ride them, get on top of them and determine their life style; but that the speaker is not one of these people. He is someone who can overcome and influence the world around him and continue to do so over a lengthy period. Such an ability is much prized in our society; and he may take much pride in it. This pride is one of many possible good feelings which may be aroused by such a self-image. It is clear how competence images and happiness images may have developed side by side for this ill person.

The third image of competence and control I want to examine here is one developed, gradually, by a woman with cancer who was following a regimen of chemotherapy prescribed by her medical practitioner. She was finding this treatment ineffective and distressing, both physically and psychologically. When she discussed changing treatments with him and other health care professionals, they insisted that she continue with the chemotherapy. She became increasingly disturbed at the consequent interference with the quality of her life. Eventually, she found herself able to say: "I'VE MADE THE DECISION TO STOP THE CHEMOTHERAPY". The flexibility of her images allowed her to see choices which were not apparent to others. She was prepared to accept even death as a possible outcome of her action, an option not acceptable to everybody. She was also prepared to accept the responsibility for the decision which she was making. She took the role of causal agent on herself, not leaving it to the health care professionals around her. This woman has now found another form of medical treatment and she has examined many of her images of illness. So far she has remained cancer-free for eight years.

Other examples of ill people's images of competence and control now follow. They include images of oneself intending to achieve certain ends and extending effort in order to do so. They focus on the ability to do what one wants to do. Other forms of competence images which our ill people have described include beliefs in oneself as determining one's course more than the physical world of people and objects around one and allocating causal roles to oneself rather than to it. A special examination is also made of all these kinds of images as they are used in relation to the control of emotions. This is followed by a description of how images of competence and helplessness can interact in people's interpretations of illness-related events. What is known of competence images is then examined: how they may affect the development of illness and determine the rate of recovery, as well as the conditions under which they seem likely to develop. I also explore some ways of developing more of these images of choice and power.

Some Illness-Related Images of Competence

Images of competence and control which are concerned with intentions will be dealt with first. These involve wanting to do something, planning to achieve something and setting goals. For example, "I LIKE TO ORGANIZE AND PLAN THINGS TO SUIT MYSELF" is a statement about how the speaker likes to relate to her world. She likes to bring things together in ways which suit herself and to do so with some foresight. Planning is important for most people; and, as we have seen, it is not easy to do if one is ill or injured. It remains a priority, however, as this statement shows: "PROVIDED YOU CAN PLAN AHEAD YOU CAN COPE WITH JUST ABOUT ANY PROBLEM PARALYSIS BRINGS". Planning involves deciding what is essential and what is inessential, what is good coping and what is a "cop out": "I'VE GOT TO WORK OUT, NOW I'VE HAD THE STROKE, WHICH EASY THINGS ARE RUNNING AWAY FROM PROBLEMS AND WHICH I SHOULD USE TO MAKE LIFE EASIER". It becomes especially important to people during their convalescence. "MY AIM IS TO GO HOME AND PICK MYSELF UP HEALTH WISE". "MY ONE THOUGHT IS TO GET MYSELF FIT AGAIN".

Effort is necessarily involved in the fulfillment of these plans. Yet sometimes images of competence and control focus on the effort alone: "MY DAY IS A CHALLENGE, WHATEVER I AM GOING TO DO". This speaker sees himself as ready to make an effort for every new day and enjoying this effort. Few people manage to retain images of this kind once their illness or injury has struck. They tend to push these images back into the past, to use them to describe themselves then and not now: "I'VE BEEN A VERY ACTIVE SORT OF FELLOW". Others, who are also unable to see themselves as able to make much effort now, can see themselves as doing so in the future. As one elderly man with multiple problems who had earned his living as a casual labourer said: "I'LL GET OUT ON MY OWN AGAIN. I'LL BATTLE ON MYSELF, BECAUSE I'M A FIGHTER". While most of the effort described by ill people was related to their illness-related images of competence, some of it was unfortunately directed towards becoming "a good patient", for example, "I TRY NOT TO BE A

NUISANCE FOR THE NURSES".

People who are disabled by illness and injury are not always able to do what they want to do. Accomplishing day-to-day tasks which healthy people do without thinking then becomes crucial evidence of ability: "I CAN GO TO THE TOILET NORMALLY NOW". This cry of victory can be extended to the accomplishment of all the other tasks we take in our stride: "YOU CAN LIVE A NORMAL LIFE IF YOU WANT TO". It can involve rehabilitation after surgery, "I AM A QUICK RECOVERER", or the securing of home help, "NOW I AM ABLE TO PAY FOR HELP". It can be a statement of survival in the face of illness of injury: "I'M COPING, APART FROM THE INCONVENIENCE". It can involve recognition of personal responsibility: "ONLY YOU CAN GET YOURSELF OUT OF A DEPRESSION". Yet when faced with severe illness some people are able to maintain a strongly positive belief in themselves and their own capacity to transcend events. "THERE'S NOT MUCH YOU CAN'T DO IF YOU PUT YOUR MIND TO IT".

Some ill people are also still able to maintain images of themselves which involve their triumph over their physical world. "I DON'T LET THINGS GET ME DOWN" indicates an overcoming of circumstances which may have been extremely stressful. Sometimes this is because of the image ill people have of themselves. "I'M A PRETTY INDEPENDENT TYPE OF PERSON" conveys that the speaker considers herself to be relatively little influenced by others. People demonstrate such independence by the advice they give about illness to others: "DON'T LET IT RUIN YOUR LIFE". They also say of themselves: "I SWORE, WHEN I GOT HODGKIN'S DISEASE, THAT I

WASN'T GOING TO LET IT RULE ME". They recognize that physical events can be controlled to some extent by psychological ones: "YOUR ATTITUDE TO YOUR HEALTH IS IMPORTANT". And, again, triumphing in the small day-to-day things can be an integral part of an image of competence and self-control, for example: "I DIDN'T HAVE A CIGARETTE ALL DAY".

Other images of competence involve perceiving oneself to be the cause of events. This was the position sought after by this speaker: "I WANT TO BE ABLE TO DO MY OWN THING IN LIFE". Shaping their own life style was being achieved by this man who had tested as HIV-antibody positive: "I'VE LEARNED A LOT ABOUT AIDS, AND NOW I'M GOING TO MAXIMIZE MY CHANGES WITH IT, BY EATING WELL, EXCERCIZING OFTEN AND GETTING PLENTY OF REST AND RELAXATION". "I'VE TAUGHT MYSELF I CAN'T HAVE ANYTHING SWEET". An image of competence had also been achieved in this woman's management of her pain: "I'VE WEANED MYSELF OFF THE TABLETS. I DON'T LIKE THE SIDE-EFFECTS THEY ARE HAVING. I'D RATHER PUT UP WITH THE PAIN". The same theme was voiced by this frail but spritely 80 year old: "I'M NOT SENILE... AND I'M NOT DOCILE... AND I'LL DECIDE IF I'M GOING TO LOSE A LEG OR NOT". They were all saying, in effect, that although their illness was a very important element in their lives, they remained the ones in charge.

Images with this theme of self-control are not only relevant to the more concrete aspects of the lives of ill people, but to the emotional aspects also. In this sphere, images of intention are built: "I AM GOING TO KEEP A TIGHT REIN ON MY FEELINGS". Effort is expended on this kind of control too: "IF I SEE MYSELF TO BE GETTING UPSET, I CLAMP DOWN HARD UNTIL IT'S OVER". Maintaining a balance of negative and positive emotions requires considerable ability: "I'M ABLE, I FIND, TO KEEP MYSELF ON AN EVEN KEEL". Some people want to transcend their more distressing feelings altogether: "THIS OPERATION IS NO MORE TO ME THAN CUTTING MY TOE". They take personal responsibility for that kind of control: "GOOD CONTROL IS UP TO YOURSELF". Some of these forms of self-control - especially the suppression of distressing feelings - we have found to be not conducive to good recovery from illness and injury. Others - for example, the balancing of negative and positive emotions so that the former do not overwhelm people - may be a skill which ill people need to develop.

Before concluding this description of ill people's images of competence and self-control, it is appropriate for me to show how they can intertwine with images of helplessness. "YOU'VE JUST GOT TO GO ON", a statement from a man with rheumatoid arthritis, is an example of this intertwining. The external force is at work in "You're just got to..." but it results in the personal strength of persistence. A diabetic's account of his energy level, "AT TIMES I DON'T FEEL LIKE DOING ANYTHING, BUT AT TIMES I DO", contains similarly contrasting elements of passivity and power. In this statement, too, the passivity is overtaken by the power: "YOU'VE GOT TO ACCEPT THE CANCER; AND YOU'VE GOT TO FIGHT IT". Sometimes, as for this stroke victim, it is the helplessness which eventually takes over: "THE MAIN THING IS LEARNING YOUR LIMITATIONS". He still sees

182

himself as able to learn; but what he learns about is his own ability. The same pattern of interplay is apparent for a woman whose life span has already been longer than she expected and filled with rewarding experiences: "I THINK YOU DO MORE WHEN YOU HAVE DEATH IN FRONT OF YOU". Although the spectre of death was continually before her, she was accomplishing much that satisfied her.

The Implications of Images of Competence

Direct evidence about the protective role played by images of competence and self-control is, compared with that about the damaging role of images of helplessness, rare as yet, although there is evidence that the controllability of illnesses affects their outcomes (Affleck et al., 1987; Felton and Revenson, 1984; Taylor, Lichtman and Wood, 1984). I shall report the results of four more studies only. Two of these studies have examined the effects of providing increased opportunities for personal responsibility and decision-making for people hospitalized with cancer (Ashcroft, Leinster and Slade, 1986; Klagsbrun, 1970). These effects consisted of considerable improvements in their psychological states. When a similar approach was taken with elderly people in nursing homes, these effects extended to their physical states as well (Langner and Rodin, 1976). The fourth study is one which has extended the work on the effects of stress on illness which was described in Chapter 4. The number of illnesses reported by a large group of people over a one month period proved to be unrelated to the number of undesirable events they had experienced and the amount of stressful change they had undergone.

More illness was reported by the people who experienced the undesirable events which they believed to be beyond their control; and the most illness was reported by those who were uncertain about whether they could control the events that occurred (Suls and Mullen, 1981).

There is more evidence pointing to the facilitating role of images of competence and control during illness and injury. Physically illness management has been effected by images of competence in at least two ways. Diabetics with these images control their blood sugar levels better (Peyrot and McMurray, 1985); and people with chronic pain control it better (Litt, 1988; Pickett and Clum, 1982). Also, the psychological factors associated with better physical condition are affected by images of competence, as in the people with cancer who have shown less anxiety and depression (Greer and Burgess, 1987; Marks et al., 1986).

In rehabilitation people who feel they have more control over themselves and their lives improve more (Shontz, 1975). The longer ill or injured people are in rehabilitation programmes, the more likely they are to develop competence and control images (Albrecht and Higgins, 1977). People with spinal cord injuries, who have as long a rehabilitation period as anyone, have been shown to cope better if they use more images of control. This effect is not apparent soon after the injury but takes time to develop (Shadish, Hickman and Arrick, 1981). This effect has also been found over a seven-month rehabilitation period for people with a wider range of chronic illnesses and injuries. People who initially use more competence images later see themselves as achieving greater rehabilitation gains in mobility and interpersonal relationships than do those who use fewer of them (Viney and Westbrook, 1982c). The same is true for images dealing specifically with self-control. Control of emotions - that balancing act between bad and good feelings - has also been shown to be associated with better recovery from surgery than either suppressing or being overwhelmed by one's feelings (Andrew, 1970).

Many psychologists believe that people prize their images of competence at all times and will go to considerable lengths to maintain them (Glidewell, 1972). People need, in other words, to see themselves as able to cope with life. People who are ill need to see themselves as able to cope with their illness; they need to feel as if they are acting effectively in relation to it (Blumberg, Flaherty and Lewis, 1980; Mechanic, 1977). This means, in fact, that they will need to develop new coping skills to deal with some of the specific tasks which illness or injury sets for them (Adams and Lindemann, 1974). These include preparing for an uncertain future, maintaining their self-esteem and having satisfying relationships with others, as well as that all important task of maintaining their emotional equilibrium (Cohen and Lazarus, 1979; Moos and Tsu, 1977).

If seeing themselves as competent at these tasks is important to people who are ill, do they manage to do so? Some people do, for example, those scheduled for surgery for reparable problems (Gottesman and Lewis, 1982), although having to cope with post-surgical pain may reduce their feelings of competence if only temporarily (Peck, 1984). As we have seen, some think of their illness or injury as a fight or a challenge (Pritchard, 1981). Also, severely ill people have been found to resist control from others and to want to assert their own control (Thomas and Weiner, 1974). However, people who are ill use fewer images in which they present themselves as active than those who are not ill (Viney and Westbrook, 1981a). Those few who see themselves as active have had a different life style before the illness from those who do not (Viney and Westbrook, 1982a). They have had more education and higher paying jobs from which they have gained more satisfaction. They are usually married and enjoy more leisure activities. In keeping with the dominant sex role expectations of our society (Viney, 1980), men are more likely to use these more active images.

Control of their emotional balance is likely to be an important task for ill people because of the major blow which they have been struck by their illness or injury. How people build up images of themselves and their world has been described in Chapter 1. Some of these images concern their own body and some of these are very likely to be based on a belief in its indestructibility. These images of physical indestructibility can be shattered for people by illness and injury (Cassell, 1976a). Images in which they reassert control over their bodies are therefore thought to be more common when disability is observed by others to be less severe, as well as when handicap is perceived by the ill person to be less severe (Viney and Westbrook, 1982c). Such images appear to reflect ill people's control over their emotions, since when they are used often both people's anger-laden images and their happy images are fewer (Viney and Westbrook,

1984). Such control may be an important skill for ill people to acquire.

One criticism which can be made of health care professionals is that many of them have not recognized the need for ill people to have the opportunities to develop coping skills (Mechanic, 1977). Appreciation of this need and the development of techniques for this purpose have been rare (Gruen, 1975; Viney and Benjamin, 1983). However, as we saw in Chapter 6, some health care professionals are finding ways of encouraging the participation of ill people in their own care (Siegler, 1981; Simonton, Matthews-Simonton and Creighton, 1978; Turk and Genest, 1979). They are pointing to the poor psychological and physical effects of the "patient's" loss of control during certain kinds of treatments (Wellisch, Fauzy and Yager, 1978) and even during the routines of hospitalization (Taylor, 1979). Of course it is not only in the treatment of their illness that people ought to be involved as competent and responsible human beings, but in the steps taken to prevent illness before it starts (Clarke and Viney, 1979).

Developing Images of Competence

All of the illness-related images of competence and control which have been examined have had to do with personal power. This power is sometimes apparent in people's plans to deal with their illness in certain ways and sometimes in the effort they make to do so. It is apparent in the images about personal ability with which we have dealt. It has been implicit in those which have dealt with asserting oneself over one's surrounding world and with oneself as the chief causal factor in events. These elaborations of the power theme were also discussed in relation to the control invoked by ill people when they struggle to maintain their emotional equilibrium. These power images are not the opposite of helplessness images but interweave with them. The same events can be interpreted in terms of both images of competence and images of helplessness. People like to feel competent, although ill people do so less than healthy people. Their choice of competence images may be associated with better rehabilitation and even with the prevention of illness. Some suggestions for developing and using more competence images, drawn from the literature of effective techniques (Viney, Benjamin and Preston, in pressa; in pressd; Viney et al., 1985b) follow. They include people's participation in their own care and the development of skills for coping with illness and illness-related events. Some methods of self-change are presented, mainly those focussing on changes in action and thought patterns. I also call attention to the continuing need for ill and injured people to be able to tolerate passivity and to tailor their methods of self-change to their own style. A dialogue with an ill person who was well on the way to becoming her own psychologist concludes this chapter.

The first step towards participation in one's own health care should be finding out what this illness means to one, that is, what images are being built up to account for it. Recognizing how one views one's world gives people some choice about how they view it. One cannot realistically see cancer, for example, as an unmitigated blessing; but it can be viewed as a challenge, as an opportunity to test one's mettle. Nor, as some of our ill people have reminded us, is it

188

necessary to let illness take over one's life. People can themselves set the goals to be achieved. Health care professionals working with cancer sufferers have made several useful suggestions along these lines (Arnkoff, 1986; LeShan, 1977; Simonton, Matthews-Simonton and Creighton, 1978). One involves the use of determinedly positive images in which cancer cells are visualized as weak and confused and their natural bodily defences are strong and triumphing. If such images fit with one's view of the world then they may be of use; if not, they are not so likely to be used successfully. Another involves people in developing an image of their "inner guide to health". This guide may take the form of a wise old man or woman, or, for that matter, Frederick or Fredrica frog, so long as it helps to put people in touch with health-giving psychic forces within themselves of which they have been unaware (Jung, 1934; Weaver, 1973). The role of family and friends here is not great but their accepting support is welcome.

It has also been recommended that people who are severely ill or injured should be taught certain skills by professionals to help them cope with their handicaps (Mechanic, 1977). These skills lead to a heightened sense of self-eficacy (Bandura, 1984). One such skill is self-preparation. If their illness is a progressive one, people can learn to anticipate what is to come and to try out various ways of dealing with it. If they are likely to recover they can come to prepare usefully for some of the problems of their convalescence. As indicated in Chapter 3, preparation for surgery often leads to quicker recovery. People can learn to use their images of illness to anticipate effectively those events with which they will be dealing. Another skill of this kind is that of compensation. People can learn to compensate for the frustrations brought about by illness and injury. They can substitute rewards and satisfactions from one source for those which are no longer available from another. One man who was injured in a car accident hundreds of miles from his home and isolated in a hospital away from his family, friends and workmates serves as an example. He learned, for the duration of his hospital stay, to compensate for his loneliness by making friends among his fellow sufferers. He moved out of a private ward to do this; but he found this well worth doing.

Psychologists have developed a variety of techniques which people can use to change themselves (Rudestam, 1980). Those which we have dealt with so far have focussed on the emotional aspects of people's images. There are others, which can be appropriately discussed here, which are better applied to change the cognitive and behavioural manifestations of these images. The thoughts inherent in some images of illness can considerably limit the ways in which people can deal with that illness. These thoughts are expressed in language; and that language itself can be limiting. Take, for example, a woman who laces her description of herself and her illness with words like "should" and "ought". "I OUGHT TO STOP SMOKING, BUT... I SHOULD GET SOME MORE REST BUT...": she uses up a lot of energy in these exhortations but has little to show for it. Recognizing the development of these images through one's use of such language structures can lead to a wider choice of available images and so more flexible coping. Thought stopping is also a good technique for dealing with unwanted images which tend to persist (Rudestam, 1980). For example, "I'M NOT GOING TO BE ABLE TO COPE WITH THE PAIN WHEN IT STARTS AGAIN" was an image which one man was not able to get out of his mind. He was able to deal with it by abruptly dismissing it when it troubled him and substituting other more captivating images in its place.

Images also have behavioural components (Bandura, 1984). They are associated with and lead to some kinds of actions while precluding others. "WHEN I'M NERVOUS, I NEED TO SMOKE A LOT" might be one of the images promoting the smoking which an earlier speaker wanted to give up. She found that self-monitoring of her smoking was sufficient to give her more control over it, that is, through getting useful feedback by plotting on a chart the number of cigarettes she smoked in the course of a day (Rudestam, 1980). Another woman using the same approach found that she smoked more at certain times of the day and so could begin to cut down at other times. Yet another found that she needed to use self-reinforcement, that is, to make some event she found enjoyable or rewarding dependent on her achieving her goal of smoking fewer cigarettes (Rimm and Masters, 1979). She enjoyed reading detective stories in the afternoon, for example, so she permitted herself to do so only when she had "earned" it by smoking fewer cigarettes during the preceding morning.

Coping with illness through such self-instruction has been shown to be effective (Weisman and Sobel, 1979). Yet it must be remembered that it is not possible to take control of illness or injury to such an extent that people can avoid the passivity engendered by it. Coping with enforced passivity and dependency can be very difficult, especially for women who subscribe to such images as "THE DEVIL FINDS WORK FOR IDLE HANDS" or men who believe that "TO BE A MAN IS TO BE STRONG AND SELF-SUFFICIENT" (Cummings, Godfrey and Burrows, 1969). People need also to learn to recognize their own style of relating to their world, that is, the dominant themes of their images, and to use strategies which fit with this (Wallston et al., 1976). People who see themselves as competent and in control are more likely to have success with techniques which require inner resources and self-control, such as meditation. Those who continue to see essential controls as in the hands of others, or even of their illness, are more likely to get greater satisfaction through working with friends and family or through professional help (Tanck and Robbins, 1979).

This was true for Rachael T. who, in her thirties, was trying to come to terms with her need for a walking frame because of her multiple sclerosis. She had been used to taking control of her life, to making decisions. She was unmarried and had established a reputation for herself as a business woman. Yet she felt herself to be over-powered by her illness. This was so unlike her usual image of herself that she became very anxious. She was able to talk to her physician about it.

Physician: "Rachael, how do you feel about your illness?"

Rachael: "I don't know. I'm confused. I feel as if everything is getting on top of me. My sister says I ought to make arrangements to go into a nursing home. That scares me. I don't know... What do you think?"

Physician: "That may be an option you want to take at some time.

You say it frightens you. Do you think that it's a choice you might want to make now?"

Rachael (doubtfully): "No... I don't think so. But sometimes I feel I just want to give up and stop fighting the MS. To tuck myself away in a home with people around to do things for me, not having to struggle to do the simplest things like get dressed and even talk - that has its attractions for me".

Knowing something of Rachael's coping skills he reminded her of them.

Physician: "Is this the first set back you've had to deal with?"

Rachael: "No, my mother died when I was only five. I found that very hard - especially as I got older - but I learned to cope with it. In fact, I learned to turn it into an asset when I was with my friends' mothers. They all gave me some mothering".

Physician: "You were able to deal with that and even turn it to your advantage sometimes".

Rachael: "Yes. And when my first business went bust, I didn't go under with it. I started work for another company and set about making contacts and building up a nest egg until I was ready for another try on my own".

Physician: "Some good came out of these disappointments for you, then. You discovered that you had strengths and resources, that you could use to make the most of them. Do you think that might be true for you for your MS too?"

Rachael: "You're right. I can't do much about my MS, but I can do a lot about my attitude to it. I'm going to try to make the most of what's left to me. I'm still able to plan my own life. I know I'll have to take it easy now; but I don't think I need a nursing home yet. This thing can really be another challenge".

Rachael was able to reactivate some of her old images of competence and control to help her deal with her illness.

CHAPTER 11

IMAGES INVOLVING FAMILY AND FRIENDS

"This illness had made me realise what my family
and friends mean to me". (Dennis T., perforated ulcer)

When people who are ill speak of images involving their family
and friends, they often imply that they are enjoying satisfying
relationships with them (Viney and Westbrook, 1979). Here are some
statements illustrating this. The first was made by an elderly woman
with a heart condition. "I HAVE SOMEONE TO LOOK AFTER ME ALL
DAY". The kind of relationship which was important to her was a
supportive one; and she needed the support to flow from others to
herself. People, to her, were resources. They were sources of warmth
and protection. She saw others as able to be nurturant and nourishing
for her and saw them as doing so reliably. She believed the extent of
these resources to be enough for her... "all day". Although she may
have made other statements to qualify this one, as it stands she has
made a simple statement of acceptance of the availability of support
from other people.

"I'VE MET A LOT OF NICE PEOPLE IN THE HOSPITAL"
presents an image of a different kind. The type of relationship which is
in focus here is more of a friendship in which appreciation of and
admiration for others is expressed. The people referred to by this
speaker are potential sources of personal satisfaction. Enjoyment of
being with them is implied. This speaker does not differentiate
between "patients" and staff in the hospital. There are "a lot of nice
people" there. He is also describing quite a high level of enjoyment in

this remark. The other main difference from the first image examined in this chapter involves the direction of the flow of the relationship. In this case the appreciation and warmth is flowing from the man who is ill to those around him.

"WHEN I WENT TO THE PATIENT GROUPS, I REALISED THAT I WASN'T THE ONLY ONE WITH PROBLEMS" presents an image of yet a different kind. Its focus is on the sharing of experiences with others. It is a statement which might well have been made by people attending one of the self-help groups advocated at the end of Chapter 8. It expresses the experience of a link with others in the form of common threats and concerns. It also describes a change in the person speaking, since to realise "that I wasn't the only one" is to admit that she did, at one time, feel unique in this regard, as well as alone. The change from loneliness and alienation to solidarity with others is clearly a change for the better. There are other positive implications in the statement too. If I am not "the only one with problems", help may be at hand. "If others have these problems, they may know more about them than I do. They may have come to cope with them better than I have. I may be able to learn from them".

The tone of these images is unmistakably positive. This is apparent, too, in the other examples which follow. They include more images of help given by others, such as husband or wife, family member or friend, physician or nurse, to oneself. Some images in which the help flows from self to others are also available, although they are much less common. This directional flow is more frequent in images of relationships which are based on appreciation of others, in this case, by the ill person of spouse, family and health professionals. Appreciation by them of oneself is also reported. Relationships based simply on sharing are described by the ill and injured in two major forms: reports of images concerning membership of clubs and other formal organizations and of those concerning the sharing of some of the negative effects of the illness with those who are close, but not themselves ill. After I have dealt with a range of such images, I consider some of their implications for illness: the role of supportive relationships in its incidence and prevention, the more specific role of the family and the extent to which these forces are being put to work to promote better health and better living with illness. This last chapter about positive images of illness closes, as have those before it, with some suggestions about how to develop more of those images.

Some Images of Illness Involving Family and Friends

Images involving help from others have been reported by the people we interviewed. Two examples will suffice: "MY WIFE IS ALWAYS THERE WHEN I NEED HER" and "MY HUSBAND HELPS ME A LOT". Similar images involving the wider family and friends are also common. Sometimes they are concerned with getting what used to be considered to be simple chores done: "MY FAMILY HELP ME WITH MY SHOPPING". Sometimes they are concerned with some aspect of the illness. As one diabetic said: "MY FRIENDS ARE VERY HELPFUL ABOUT MY INJECTIONS. THEY KEEP AN EYE ON ME".

Sometimes they express a more general sense of support, as in this statement of strength and comfort: "IT IS GOOD TO KNOW THAT THE FAMILY IS BEHIND ME WHEN I AM ILL". Helpful images may also involve nurses and physicians as the source of good things. "THE NURSE SHOWED ME THE KIND OF DIET I SHOULD STICK TO", as a man hospitalized for gall stone removal said. "THE DOCTOR HAS DONE ME A LOT OF GOOD THIS TIME" was the pleased comment of a woman leaving hospital after her seventh piece of surgery in as many years. Another statement of thanks came from a man whose ailment was still not adequately diagnosed: "AT LEAST THE HOSPITAL HAS SUCCEEDED IN MAKING ME FEEL BETTER".

Much less common, as I have noted, are images of help in which ill people see themselves as the source of that help and the giver of it to others. A few stalwarts, however, hang on to some of the helpful roles they have played before their illness or injury. Some men do so, for example: "I CAN STILL DO THE SHOPPING FOR MY WIFE". Women do so somewhat more frequently, perhaps because aiding others is such an important aspect of their role in our society (Carlson and Kanter, 1975). "WHEN THE CHILDREN COME IN TO THE HOSPITAL, I GET THEM TO TELL ME ALL THEIR LITTLE PROBLEMS". "I WORRY ABOUT HOW THE FAMILY IS GETTING ON WITHOUT ME TO SMOOTH THINGS OVER". "I AM ONLY HAPPY WHEN I AM DOING SOMETHING THAT MIGHT HELP SOMEONE ELSE". To be the helping one in a relationship is difficult for ill people but not impossible. What seems to be even more difficult is for them to join with others in mutually helpful enterprises. I have not known any hospitalized person to use an image, for example, which includes himself or herself and health care professionals working supportively together towards the common goal of his or her better health. The professional members of the health care team may employ such images; but their "patients" do not.

Images containing appreciation and affection, on the other hand, are often focussed so that the flow is from the ill person to others. Spouses are often valued highly at this time of crisis: "MY HUSBAND IS VERY GOOD TO ME" and "I HOPE THE CHILDREN DON'T PUT TOO GREAT A LOAD ON THE WIFE WHILE I'M IN HOSPITAL". Of course, sometimes the grounds for appreciation are not what one might expect. One man, realizing how much he looked forward to his wife's visit each day but somewhat embarrassed by this, couched his approval in these terms: "I'VE GOT A GOOD COOK AT HOME, YOU KNOW". The wider family come to be valued highly too. "I DO LOVE THOSE CHILDREN". "I JUST LIVE FOR MY FAMILY". Even more distant family members, who may not have been held in much esteem before the illness, can now be seen in a more positive light: "EVEN MY MOTHER-IN-LAW HAS BEEN PRETTY GOOD TO ME SINCE I HAVE HAD THESE PROBLEMS".

Other sources of personal satisfaction emerge outside the family. One of these is friends. "I'VE GOT A VERY NICE FRIEND. SHE'S A REAL BACKSTOP", for example, shows the way in which a supportive friend may be valued. "I HAVE MET SOME WONDERFUL PEOPLE

THROUGH OUR AIDS SUPPORT GROUP". Ill people also seem to be aware of changes stimulated by their illness in images of good relationships, for example: "THIS ILLNESS HAS MADE ME REALIZE WHAT MY FRIENDS AND FAMILY MEAN TO ME". Another is the group of health care professionals with whom ill and injured people come into contact. Images of this kind are common. "DR. _____, HE'S A VERY NICE MAN". "DR. _____ IS A REALLY GOOD DOCTOR". "THE SISTERS AND NURSES ARE WONDERFUL". "SISTER _____, SHE'S MY FAVOURITE". Often, as with friends, it is the support of the nurses and physicians which is prized, rather than their expertise. "I ALWAYS TRY TO COME BACK TO THIS HOSPITAL", as one lady with considerable experience of hospitals said, "BECAUSE THEY ARE SO FRIENDLY HERE".

Knowing that one is, oneself, a source of personal satisfaction to others can also be important to ill people. This woman with multiple sclerosis was speaking of all her family could possibly do for her in this statement: "MY FAMILY IS VERY UNDERSTANDING. THEY KNOW WHEN I HAVE MY BAD DAYS; AND THEY GIVE ME A LOT OF LOVE THEN". Other families are said to show their love in other ways: "THE FAMILY WILL BE GLAD TO GET ME HOME". Friends are seen as loving too: "THE CANCER HAS SHOWN ME THAT I HAVE SO MANY FRIENDS WHO CARE ABOUT ME". Love from others develops into a burdensome image too: "I'M CONCERNED ABOUT BRINGING WORRY TO THE PEOPLE WHO LOVE ME". Nurses and doctors are not often, of course, seen as sources of love; but they can be seen as appreciating one's efforts towards better health and rehabilitation: "THE NURSES LIKE ME TO WORK HARD ON GETTING MY ARM BACK INTO SHAPE" and "THE DOCTOR IS VERY PLEASED WITH MY PROGRESS". Like images of help, few images of appreciation and affection are couched by ill people in terms which portray oneself included with others in expressing satisfaction about a relationship. Only one kind of example comes to mind, one expressing mutually rewarding intimacy with family or friends: "MY ILLNESS HAS BROUGHT US CLOSER TOGETHER".

Shared relationships, without overtones of aid or intimacy, are more often expressed as including oneself with others. These can be images focussing on membership of social organizations, for example, "I STILL GO TO THE CLUB" and "WITH THE SEWING GROUP, YOU GET OUT OF YOURSELF". This latter image conveys the transcending of one's own private concerns and problems which can occur when one is enjoying oneself with other people. The image of sharing more common among people who are ill is, however, one which focusses on the negative effects of the illness and the unavoidability of sharing them. "WE'VE GOT TO GIVE AND TAKE WITH EACH OTHER MORE NOW" is one. "WE CAN'T PLAN TO GO ANYWHERE NOW" is another. This sharing of deprivation brought about by illness and injury is mentioned frequently by those we have interviewed: "WE USED TO TRAVEL ALL OVER THE COUNTRY. NOW...". Those healthy people who are closest are most likely to share the suffering of illness or injury: "THIS HEART ATTACK HAS TAKEN A LOT OUT OF EVERYONE IN

THE FAMILY".

Images which describe oneself as initiating an interaction of this kind with others often involve communication about the illness. One young woman, whose medical practitioner had just told her of her diabetes, reported: "I WENT STRAIGHT HOME AND RANG MY MOTHER TO TELL HER ABOUT IT". A young man, who was in the initial stages of coming to terms with a diagnosis of multiple sclerosis, voiced this as his chief concern: "I HAVE TALKED TO MY WIFE ABOUT IT; BUT I'M NOT SURE SHE UNDERSTANDS WHAT IT IS GOING TO MEAN FOR US". Images involving initiation of simple, sharing relationships by others - unlike those for support and intimacy images - are not common. Images involving visits by others to the hospital are the only examples that I have found: "THE PEOPLE I WORK WITH HAVE BEEN IN TO SEE ME". If people who are hospitalized want to establish shared relationships which are not specifically supportive or appreciative, they seem to need to play the initiating role themselves. That is the picture which their images convey.

Some ill people are blessed by images which indicate that they are experiencing many satisfying interpersonal relationships. This man, suffering from rheumatoid arthritis in his late sixties, was such a person. He needed help from others to perform the most minor of physical activities, and he had become able to accept this help without undue shame or frustration: "MY WIFE HELPS ME SHOWER AND DRESS". He loved his wife for this, as for the other parts of their lives they had shared; and he felt content in her love for him: "I'VE GOT THE BEST LITTLE WIFE IN THE WORLD; AND SHE THINKS THE SAME OF ME". He was also able to respect and have faith in the health care professionals who have worked with him. "I'M IN GOOD HANDS WITH DR. _____". "WHEN I HAVE TO GO INTO HOSPITAL, THE NURSES ARE VERY PATIENT WITH ME". He has also continued to use images about relationships in which he has been involved with other people, especially through formal organizations. "I HAVE BEEN PRESIDENT OF THIS CLUB AND THAT CLUB. I STILL BELONG TO THEM AND ENJOY GOING DOWN TO MEET SOME OF MY OLD FRIENDS". This man was thinking of himself as embedded in a supportive network of family, professionals and friends. Was this likely to affect the progress of his illness?

Some Implications of Images Involving Family and Friends

These images of satisfying interaction with others may have some protective function for people who are ill. There is evidence that people, like the man who has just been described, may suffer less severe symptoms from their illness than those who do not believe themselves to be so fortunate (Luborsky, Todd and Katcher, 1978). There are also data available which suggest that the lasting physical effects of a disease like rheumatoid arthritis may be less severe if one is aware of the support available from good relationships (Lin et al., 1979). With a chronic disease, like this one, total relief of symptoms is very unlikely to occur. The quality of life which chronically ill people experience, therefore, is likely to be more dependent on the quality of the close relationships available to them than on their physical state (Eii, 1985-86; McFarlane, et al., 1984; Mechanic, 1977). Relationships can be improved, while physical states may not be able to be.

For people whose illnesses are not necessarily chronic, having many positive images of relationships with family and friends may be linked with better recovery from illness-related symptoms (Weisman and Worden, 1975). This is true for accident victims, for example, who are more quickly rehabilitated if good relationships are available to them (Bulman and Wortman, 1977; Porritt, 1977). This also appears to be true for people with heart disease, where physical recovery is possible (Doehrman, 1977). Similar information is available about the physical symptoms of cancer (Weisman and Worden, 1976-77). Coping with cancer also seems to be aided by positive interpersonal relationships, whether it be in the initial stages of diagnoses (Carey, 1974) or later, when people are close to death (Bloom, 1986; Bloom and Speigel, 1984; Jamison, Wellisch and Pasnau, 1978). Confirmation of these findings with all of these illnesses and injuries is available (Viney and Westbrook, 1982c). People who report many images of relationships are likely to show better rehabilitation, especially in terms of mobility, than those who report few of them.

As with some of the other images explored here, there is information available which suggests that images of positive interactions with family and friends may have a protective effect. People who have many such images may be more healthy. They complain of fewer health problems (Kaplan, Cassel and Gore, 1977). They also report fewer problems that are eventually diagnosed as psychosomatic disorders, that is, those disorders which, while causing very real physiological damage, have their origins in mental rather than physical events (Cassel, 1976b). They may also be less likely to suffer from fewer specific organ impairments, such as heart disease, or at least have organs, such as the heart, which are able to resist disease for longer (Lynch, 1977). This protective effect of images of positive interactions is probably the result of their modifying peoples other reactions to stress (Hartsfield and Clopton, 1985; Hobfoll and Walfisch, 1984; McKay et al., 1985).

The family members are those to whom, for many ill people, the ties are the closest and strongest. While this is generally acknowledged, some of the implications of this state of affairs are not well recognized. For example, if images involving family members are so important during recovery and may even participate in preventing illness, they may also be involved in developing illness (Proctor, 1985). Yet people after heart attacks who are struggling to make sense of what has happened to them do not consider this factor. They attribute their illness to smoking or even stress at work; stress amongst the family does not apparently cross their minds as a cause (Koslowsky, Kroog and La Voie, 1978). Nor is it recognized that, for people who are too disabled to continue to go out to work, family relationships must replace relationships with workmates. This puts a lot of responsibility on family members; and if some of the relatively few relationships available within the family are not rewarding, the level of stress within the family is likely to rise. Yet another aspect of a person's illness in the context of their family to which sufficient attention has not yet been paid is its psychological impact on that family. Severe illness or injury creates stress for other family members (Skelton and Dominian, 1973). They need to get in touch with and express their feelings, just as ill people themselves need to do (Blumberg, Flaherty and Lewis, 1980). And ill people need to strike a balance when relying on family and other support networks (Gottlieb, 1985).

If images of positive relationships with family and friends are so central to the well-being of ill people, do they find it easy to maintain these images in the face of the isolation and loneliness induced by their illness and subsequent hospitalization? The answer to this question, put simply, is no. Ill people do like to talk to others about their physical problems at times, but they do not appear to do so consistently (Pritchard, 1981). Sharing problems with others is a common enough strategy for people to use when dealing with other kinds of crises (Bazeley and Viney, 1977; Ilfield, 1980; Tanck and Robbins, 1979). However, it seems that it is used relatively rarely by people who are chronically ill (Viney and Westbrook, 1984). Of course this use may differ from person to person. There do appear to be differences in how men and women react to stress (Gleser and Ihilevich, 1969; Haan, 1977), and there may be when they are dealing with illness (Kessler, 1979; Westbrook and Viney, 1983). When coping with imminent surgery, for example, women express their anxious, angry and depressed images more readily than men, although the men may be experiencing more discomfort than they admit (Weiss, 1969). Men are expected, in our society, to present a "stiff upper lip". Women are permitted more freedom to share their inadequacies and discomforts with others (Viney, 1980; Viney et al., 1985).

The reader has already been introduced to the twin concepts of disability and handicap as they are used in this volume. Both have to do with limitations on what ill or injured people are able to do for themselves. Disability is observed from an external perspective and indicates the extent of the limitations observed by others. Handicap is experienced from an internal perspective by the ill person on his own limitations. Both bear some relationship to whether positive images of family and friends are experienced often by ill people or not. The less severe the disability, especially in the area of mobility, the more of these images they are likely to report (Viney and Westbrook, 1981a). The less severe the handicap, the more they report of these images also; but in this case it is perceived limitations in that all important area of maintaining relationships, as well as in self-care which is important.

Developing More Images Involving Family and Friends

Various images focussing on positive relationships with family and friends have been examined. They have included helpful relationships between lovers, family and friends, and the ill person and the professionals caring for him or her. These images of help collected from ill people have focussed on both relationships initiated by ill people and relationships initiated by others. They have not focussed on joint involvement in such relationships. This joint involvement in more intimate relationships has also been rare; although many images involving oneself in prizing others or others in prizing oneself have been explored. Shared experiences have proved to be more often undergone jointly, especially when people are referring to the negative consequences their illness have for their family and close friends together with themselves. In their images they initiate some sharing experiences themselves; but very little of this is thought of as generated by others. It seems that all of these kinds of images help promote quicker rehabilitation and recovery from illness as well as protecting people from the more severe symptoms of illness or even the illness itself. The family may be particularly important here. It is a pity, then, that ill and injured people do not use more of these images than they do. The uniqueness of some symptoms and injuries and the flavour of the hospital milieu may work against such use. That is why I close this chapter with an exploration of why it is difficult for families and very close friends to provide the interpersonal support which is lacking from many images of illness and some suggestions about how they can do so. Some ways for counsellors to work with families and friends are also discussed. Finally, I suggest that some alienation from these relationships occurs because of the self-limiting nature of the images of ill people. An example of this alienation is provided.

One way in which it is difficult for family and friends to respond well to people who have become ill is that they are responding to, at least initially, the illness itself for which they are likely to have images generating very negative feelings. These feelings need to be dealt with before they can relate to the ill person (Benoliel, 1974). Another is that there are certain barriers to that relationship; not the least of which are their own images about how they ought to act when visiting a severely ill person (Reiss, 1981). The determinedly cheerful visitor can provide a strong barrier to meaningful communication, as Gordon M. indicated (in Chapter 8). These kinds of barriers can lead family and friends to avoid all discussions of the illness or to avoid the illness altogether by avoiding the ill person (Greer and Moorey, 1987). It can also lead to some confusing discrepancies between what visitors say and what they actually communicate (Wortman and Dunkel-Schetter, 1979). This lack of communication has not often been dealt with by health care professionals, who themselves sometimes tend to avoid contact with family and friends where possible (Straus, 1975). Sometimes, then, it is necessary for ill people themselves to initiate the type of interaction they want, making it very clear to others what their roles are to be.

Friends and families of people who are severely ill who are reading this book will now be asking: how can I develop a more supportive relationship with the ill person I love? There are listening and responding skills which can be acquired with practice (Guerney, 1977; Gendlin, 1981). This process starts with the feelings of the friend or family member and goes on to the feelings of the ill person. These feelings are an integral part of the images all of these people are using to make sense of the illness and its consequences. They must be recognized and expressed in order to prevent them from distorting communication. What both people will be aiming to establish is effective, as well as open communication (Benoliel, 1974; Simonton, Matthews-Simonton and Creighton, 1978). Openness comes through honesty. If this kind of communication is difficult to achieve, then counselling from a professional may be the answer. Certainly family and friends should try to support "patients" in more active participation in their own care which I have suggested; and they should try to get as much relevant information as possible from the health care professionals. Well-informed relatives or friends can be very supportive to ill people during their convalescence. They can even come to take a role as active members of the health care team (Pratt, 1976; Wellisch, Mosher and Van Scoy, 1978).

A few words on the counselling of friends and relatives may be helpful here. It has been shown to be useful to work with relatives to reduce their images of uncertainty and anxiety by providing them with information about the ill or injured person (Bunn and Clarke, 1979). However, to do this without frequent consultation with the ill person may be of limited value. I would reiterate here that there should be no withholding of information from the person who is ill, that is, no secrecy. Nor should the counsellor be lured into being the go-between for ill people and their families, since the aim of the counselling is to produce open and effective communication between them without either help or interference from others. It may be that the best counselling involves the counsellor in working simultaneously with the ill person and their family (Viney, Benjamin and Preston, in pressb) as in, for example, the groups which have been run for stroke victims and their families (D'Afflitti and Weitz, 1974).

That positive images of family and friends have been maintained by some ill people, has more to do, sometimes, with their already existing images of others than how those others act. Take, for instance, a mother whose image of her four-year old was as follows: "LISA IS ALWAYS WELL-BEHAVED WHEN WE ARE OUT". Lisa's behaviour when she came "out" to the hospital then troubled her mother a good deal. Lisa sometimes acted as if she did not know her mother, at others she wanted to climb all over her, including the most painful parts of her body. When the time comes for leaving, Lisa did not want to go and threw a tantrum in order to make this clear. Her mother was upset by these events and complained: "I DON'T KNOW WHAT'S GOT INTO LISA. I DON'T UNDERSTAND HER". It was her hanging on to that earlier image which made her understanding difficult. If her mother had been able to alter that image of her daughter's public behaviour in a place where she found her mother different, the hospital strange and was beset by the nagging fear that her mother would never come back to her, she would not have become alienated from her daughter.

Mollie G. and her husband provide an illustration of how a dominant image which is interfering with communication among family members can be altered through the intervention of a counsellor.

Mollie was hospitalized, in her forties, for repairs following the hysterectomy which she had had six years earlier. The repairs had eventually become necessary because she had hurled herself too soon and too strenuously into looking after her husband and three teenage sons and contributing to the family business. The image which dominated the whole family in its relationships with her was: "GOOD WOMEN LOOK AFTER OTHER PEOPLE". Mollie had accepted this image but, with the help of a counsellor, was able to modify it. For her, it had become something more like: "GOOD WOMEN CARE FOR - THAT IS, LOVE - OTHER PEOPLE". The problem she found with her family was one of getting them to accept that she could show her love to them in ways other than doing all their laundry for them. The counsellor agreed with Mollie that she would see her husband in order to prepare the way for this change. Tim G. was hesitant at first:

Tim: "I don't know what I can do. Shouldn't you be talking to my wife?"

Counsellor: "I have talked with your wife; and she has told me a lot about how she feels about all of you and about being ill. She loves the family very much - doesn't she?"

Tim: "Yes, she does. She's always busy doing things for us".

Counsellor: "And you love her too..."

Tim: "Well, it's not the kind of thing a man says much about. But yeah..."

Counsellor: "And you worry about her..."

Tim: "She does too much for the boys. I think I'll speak to them about that. The youngest is 16 now. They all ought to be able to make their own beds. They'll have to pull their weight around the house now".

Counsellor: "That sounds like a good idea. And what about helping her to feel loved too? What can you all do about that?"

Tim: "The boys can make a fuss of her... I suppose I could too... You know... It's been a while since she and I have had some fun together. It's mostly been work, work, work... What can I do about that?"

Counsellor: "What do you think?"

Tim: "... er... I might just tell her straight out what I think".

Counsellor: "Good! And you could also do some planning with her about how you two can spend some free time together".

Tim: "That sounds good too".

Needless-to-say, Mollie was very pleased when her husband made this suggestion to her during his next visit to the hospital. Together they made plans which resulted in a more gradual recuperation for her this time.

SECTION 4

REFLECTIONS

This section contains my reflections on the findingsfrom our research into images of illness. The approach we took and the methods we adopted hopefully have led to a greater understanding of the richness and variety of people's images. The research has also identified some common, shared images and shown how they are constructed by people from their experience of illness-related events. In so doing, it has high-lighted ways in which people dealing with illness are able to choose between many interpretations of illness-related events and how health professionals working with them, as well as their relatives and friends, can help them widen the range of images of illness available to them.

CHAPTER 12

UNDERSTANDING PEOPLE'S IMAGES OF ILLNESS

"Both in living and in inquiry within psychology,

we need to develop ways in which we may be

more sensitive to and respectful towards the

diverse ways in which we and others fashion

the styles of the realities in which we live".

(Mair, 1976, p. 286)

My purpose in writing this last chapter is to reflect on the results

of the psychological research which have been presented here. I will

examine the major assumptions of the research, for example, the

importance of illness images in the lives of people suffering illness, the

role of these people as interpreters of their own experience of

illness-related events and the power which has accrued to their

images. These images of illness are more influential than they might

be because of our lack of awareness, both of their content and of their

status as created images rather than given realities. The effectiveness

of the methodology chosen to identify these images will also be

discussed.

I will also reflect on some of the findings from the research: the

complexity and richness of the images and the variety of images

identified even for a single form of illness. What we have learned

about how images of illness are constructed will be considered,

together with the ways in which they can be expanded or constricted

according to the needs of the people who develop them. Some attention will also be paid to how images can remain stable over time and, in some cases, are protected at considerable cost, and how others are more amenable to change. Some of the implications of these images of illness for illness and health will be explored. I will also examine the implications of the images of illness developed by people other than those who are ill themselves, that is, by their family and friends and the health care professionals who work with them.

The Importance of Images of Illness : The Assumptions and Aims of this Research

This research was begun with the assumption that one important form of reality is what people believe it to be. It is through their images of it that we gain access to that reality. My images are what I believe to be true; your images are what you believe to be true (Boulding, 1974). It follows that we can ourselves determine this form of reality and so have control over it (Gordon, 1972). Society validates or confirms some of our images more readily than others (Berger and Luckman, 1972). Personal experience of illness also validates some images more readily than others (Kelly, 1955). These assumptions have provided a fruitful basis for the research which has been reported. We have been able to learn how people interpret illness-related events for themselves and, as psychologists, we have tried to understand their interpretations or images.

People act according to their interpretations of reality (Kelly,1955). Ill people who have not developed images of their illness are therefore not only confronted with meaninglessness but have no frame of reference within which to take action. Ill people try hard, therefore, to interpret their symptoms (Cowie, 1976). They attribute cause and effect to the events they associate with their illness or injury (Bulman and Wortman, 1977; Janis and Rodin, 1979). "IF THAT DAMN RAIN HAD NOT COME PELTING DOWN ALL OF A SUDDEN, I NEVER WOULD HAVE THE ACCIDENT" is an example of an anger-laden image in which such attribution is apparent. As I have reported elsewhere (Viney, 1983), I can find evidence for this need for meaning as a basis for action in my own attempts to deal with an illness as mild as the common cold. When I have a cold and happen to meet someone who has had one recently, I find myself asking them to share their symptoms with me. "Mine started in my throat". "So did mine". "Now mine seems to have moved up into my nose". "How long did you have yours?" "I was in bed for five days". "Well, at least I haven't succumbed to bed... yet". This kind of dialogue, together with my reflection on the colds I have had in the past, makes it possible for me to identify this cold among the many images of colds available to me and to predict its likely course. The extent to which we experience the power to deal with an illness, as for any source of stress, depends on whether we can create these kinds of images (Thompson, 1981).

Images of illness, together with images of death, are rarely discussed in our society (van den Berg, 1980). It has been a lack of full awareness of their content, together with lack of recognition that these images do not necessarily represent the events of the real world accurately, which have given these images a power which sometimes surpasses the power of those who have created them. Identifying some of these images and clarifying the role of ill people in constructing them should give some power back to those people through the choices it gives them. Those are the aims of this work. This book contains both descriptions of many images of illness and of ways of dealing with them. Humour is one important way. Through humour, people can comment on the relationship between different images of reality. This strategy has been used by ill people (Coser, 1959), like the diabetic who joked about feeling like an exhausted marathon runner after an ordinary day's work. They can control the relationship between image and reality, as did the young man who created, in fantasy, his own flirtatious bear. They can also use humour to develop images which come closer to reality, as Andy's counsellor did when she helped him come to terms with his paraplegia.

Identifying Images: The Method

A research method which would enable identification of some of the images of illness which ill people use was needed. This research has been a search for patterns, in this case patterns representing images. In research as well as life we need to find ways of "tuning in" other people's images (Mair, 1970). We have enlisted the cooperation of the ill people who participated in the research, telling them of our aims and asking them to give us accounts of their current experiences (Kelly, 1965; Harre and Secord, 1972). Our interviewers were able to help them to feel comfortable in this role. The interviewers also found the open-ended question they asked them to be a fruitful one. This question had as little structure as possible, so as to introduce our images and expectations of the researchers as little as possible.

Our aim has been to identify images from the responses of the research participants; we have not made inferences about images which have not been part of the social reality we have shared with them. We have used content analysis of their responses to "tune in" their images. We have been, I believe, successful in achieving our aims. We have interviewed a group of ill people who, as well as including both men and women, and people who are married and not married, has represented a wide range of educational and occupational status and many different types of illness. In spite of these differences, many of the patterns we found, which enabled us to identify images of illness, were common to many people (Viney, in pressb). Some of our research findings will now be examined.

Some Findings from the Research

The findings I now want to explore are the complexity and richness of the images, the differences among images generated by similar illness-related events, how images are constructed and how they lead to expansion and constriction of one's view of the world. Let me deal with the complexity of images first. Regardless of the emotion associated with each image of illness, their meaning has proved to be even richer than we initially recognized. The old man, who considered that he should "accept" the uncertainties of his illness rather than "cope" with them, saw "acceptance" not so much as a weak and passive reaction but a strong and enduring one. The younger man who said, in relation to his illness, "I'VE BEEN UNDER A LOT OF STRESS LATELY", while admitting to anxiety was seeing it as part of a complex causal pattern. Similarly, this anger-laden image "I AM FED UP WITH BEING SICK ALL THE TIME" does not stop at conveying the speaker's experience of never-ending disability but adds to it the frustrations such a plight can cause. The same richness of meaning can be observed in some of the less distressing images, "I'VE GOT ANOTHER WRINKLE; AND THAT SHOWS I'VE LIVED ANOTHER YEAR. THAT'S TERRIFIC" describes a complex reaction to an event usually viewed negatively. "ONLY YOU CAN GET YOURSELF OUT OF A DEPRESSION" shows an interplay of positive and negative emotions.

It has been maintained that there are as many alternative perspectives on events as there are people to take perspectives (Kelly, 1955). This has proved to be the case for perspectives on illness too. An examination of the images used by people with multiple sclerosis, to take just one example, which have been described in this volume show this to be true. They include at least one image of uncertainty, "WHAT AM I GOING TO TELL MY HUSBAND ABOUT IT?", and another of anxiety, "I CAN SEE MYSELF GETTING UPSET ABOUT THINGS AT HOME. IT DOESN'T DO ME MUCH GOOD". It has also prompted anger-laden images: "THERE ARE SILLY PEOPLE WHO THINK THEY

HAVE TO DO EVERYTHING FOR ME". Other images employed by sufferers of multiple sclerosis have included helplessness, "EVERYTHING IS GETTING A BIT MUCH FOR ME", depression, "MY DEPRESSION IS HARDER TO DEAL WITH THAN MY ILLNESS" and isolation, "THE LONELINESS IS THE WORST THING". Moreover, people with multiple sclerosis can also maintain more pleasant images, "UNTIL YOU ARE ILL, YOU DON'T REALLY APPRECIATE THE GOOD THINGS IN LIFE", including those indicating a sense of personal competence, "I TRY TO KEEP MYSELF ALERT AND INTERESTED IN THE WORLD OUTSIDE" and of helpful relationships, "MY FAMILY IS VERY UNDERSTANDING, THEY KNOW WHEN I HAVE MY BAD DAYS; AND THEY GIVE ME A LOT OF LOVE THEN". Ill people can differ greatly in the images they choose. Yet there are many images which they share in spite of the different kinds of illness-related events which they face. These are anxiety-laden and anger-laden images and images of helplessness and depression, as well as happy images (Westbrook and Viney, 1982).

Another gain from this research has been a greater understanding of how images are constructed through the interaction of image-makers with their real world of people and objects. Images of illness are often the product of interaction between ill people and their illness. "I GET ANGRY AND DEPRESSED BY THESE SETBACKS" is the product of the speaker's hopes and fears and the results of those hopes and fears about the course of her illness over a long period of time. Illness-related images can also be constructed by people after a period of interaction with others of which some aspect of their illness is the focus: "THERE'S NOTHING WORSE THAN BEING MADE TO FEEL TOTALLY USELESS". It is not only distressing images which are created in this way, but more pleasant ones too. "I'VE BEEN A VERY ACTIVE SORT OF FELLOW" conveys a view of oneself built up in this way. So, too, does this image which was developed to give meaning to someone else's actions rather than one's own: "I'VE GOT A VERY NICE FRIEND. SHE'S A REAL BACKSTOP".

Yet another important finding has been how images, because of their implications, help to expand people's perspective on the reality of their lives while others constrict it. These images have the property of promoting expansion: "MY PHILOSOPHY OF LIFE IS THAT NOTHING IS IMPOSSIBLE" and "MY DAY IS A CHALLENGE, WHATEVER I AM GOING TO DO". It is no coincidence that these are images of competence. Yet even ill people who feel helpless are not prevented from expanding their images, as Elizabeth showed when she moved from an image of herself as "a good patient" to that of a participant in her own treatment. In contrast, these images promote constriction and a narrow view of reality: "I AM USELESS" and "HEALTHY PEOPLE DON'T UNDERSTAND WHAT IT IS LIKE TO BE ILL". The first image cuts its creator off from her own resources; and the second cuts its creator off from many people who could help her. It is no coincidence that these are images of depression and isolation. Anger, too, can be constricting if handled inappropriately, as we have seen with Jean who needed a counsellor's help to express it.

Stable and Changing Images of Illness

Some images remain relatively stable; others are more easily altered. People tend to hang on to their old images even though they do not serve them well. Images which are of central importance to one's perspective on the world are especially resistant to change (Kelly, 1955). An image of someone very close, as in Lisa's mother's image of her young daughter's "behaviour" when "out", can be resistant to change. Many of people's most important images have to do with themselves. It is self-images, therefore, which are often maintained in the face of evidence to the contrary. This was true for the man whose eyes teared when his veins were being probed: "I DON'T CRY IN PUBLIC. EVEN WHEN MY WIFE DIED I DIDN'T DO THAT". It was also true for Richard, the relatively young heart attack victim, who wanted to hang on to his image of himself as "strong" even though it threatened his life. Sometimes, however, the stability of important self-images is a valuable asset, as Rachael found as she reinstated her old image of herself as competent to deal with the new events in her life introduced by multiple sclerosis.

People with images which no longer enable them to make sense of what they are experiencing can sometimes change them by setting themselves specific tasks and acquiring certain skills. This can be achieved by ill people through working as one's own counsellor. Georgia did this with success when she learned how to relax at will her neck and shoulder muscles. Such a change is often easier, however, if people are working in the kind of dialogue that has been illustrated at the end of each of the chapters of Sections 2 and 3 of this book. A professional counsellor can develop such a relationship with an ill person; but it can also be provided by others who are empathic and skillful such as health care professionals, or even family and friends. The woman who complained "I'M ALWAYS THINKING ABOUT ME. I'VE NEVER BEEN LIKE THAT BEFORE", was in need of such a helpful interaction. The woman who said "HEALTHY PEOPLE DON'T KNOW WHAT IT IS LIKE TO BE ILL" learned from an empathic but never-the-less healthy listener to change her constricting and distorting image. George, who had been avoiding his surgery for haemorrhoids, was able to change his image of the effects of anaesthetics through such a dialogue. Sometimes dialogue is necessary because people's images tend to be intertwined with those of people close to them. Mollie's husband had to change his image of her, for example, so that she could act on the basis of her image of herself as a loving wife and mother rather than as a faithful maid of all work. Perhaps the most memorable dialogue of this kind reported here was between Richard and his counsellor, during which Richard came to see his "cowardly" concerns about his heart as something he could "bravely" share with his wife.

The Implications of Some Images of Illness

The implications of illness images can be explored in terms of individual images or in terms of types of images. Let me look at some implications of individual images first, beginning with some of the more distressing ones. "ALL MY CHILDREN WILL TELL YOU THAT I HAVE HAD A COMPLETE PERSONALITY CHANGE SINCE THE ILLNESS". This image reflects its speaker's uncertainty about who she is and the uncertainty she believes others experience with her. It implies that she is changing and unpredictable, with her only certainty being that she is not the person she was before. The implications of this anxiety-laden image are very different: "I'LL BE SCARED UNTIL THIS OPERATION IS OVER". It recognizes an unpleasant emotion but also what has generated it; and, most important, it implies that the emotion will pass. "I'M GOING TO BATTLE TO GET A SECOND MEDICAL OPINION" is an anger-laden image which implies that the world is hostile and will not easily grant the speaker what she wants. Of course the world may not be like that; her physician may be eager for her to have another opinion. "IT'S TOO LATE TO CHANGE NOW" is a helpless image of lost opportunity. This research participant believed she had no choice in how she acted. This is one of the implications, too, of this depression-laden image: "I'VE LOST ALL INTEREST IN LIFE". The implications of this image of isolation are also worth noting: "IF I'M NOT LOVED BY SOMEBODY, I'M NOBODY". The young woman who said this was aware that if she could not feel lovable, she could have little sense of self-worth. In this, she was probably right.

Whether the implications of these images represent shared reality accurately or distort it, they are far-reaching in their effects. The implications of these images laden with distressing emotion have tended to be somewhat negative. In contrast, those of positively-toned images have been found to be more positive. General good humour is implicit in this image: "I'VE GOT A PRETTY HAPPY NATURE". It suggests that its creator is often cheerful, even without any special effort by him to remain so, and that, if there is a silver lining to the clouds of his illness, he will find it. This is another self-image which implies strength: "I'M NOT THE KIND OF PERSON WHO GIVES IN TO ILLNESS". This statement reflects a belief in one's own ability to cope. Finally, I have selected as an example an image which is overtly positive in tone but has some negative implications: "I CAN STILL DO THE SHOPPING FOR MY WIFE". This man, in spite of his illness, has been able to continue in his helpful role with his wife. What is implicit are the forces which are working against this in the form of his weakness or increasing disability, together with the fear that he will not be able to continue much longer.

Do positively toned and negatively toned images of illness differ in their implications for the health of the people using them? The answer is yes, but not always quite as might be expected. Of the six distressing types of images which our research participants have shared with us, three appear to have consistently negative implications. Uncertainty-laden images, and images of helplessness and isolation can all be constructed in response to illness and injury. They tend to make people more vulnerable to illness; and they work against their rehabilitation and recovery. The other three negatively-toned images - images laden with anxiety, anger and depression - are characteristic of people's reactions to illness and injury and also may make them more vulnerable. These images differ, however, from the first group in promoting rehabilitation and recovery, so long as they are identified and expressed by the people experiencing them. Anxiety, anger or depression which is hidden or ignored may be as devastating in its long term effects as any of the other distressing emotions.

The more welcome emotions have better implications for health. Images of happiness and competence, as well as those involving family and friends, have all been found to be associated with decreased vulnerability to accident and injury. They have also, in at least some studies, been found to aid rehabilitation and recovery. They differ from each other, however, in this way. Images of happiness, like those of anxiety, anger and depression have been found, consistently across a number of studies, to be characteristic of the most common pattern of emotional reaction to illness. Images implying a sense of personal competence and control and those implying good relationships with family members and friends have been found to be much less common among ill people. Since these images, too, appear to encourage health and work against illness, ill and injured people should be encouraged to develop and maintain them.

The Influence of the Images of Others on Those of Ill People

All of us influence the images of the ill people we work with or to whom we are close. Relatives of ill people differ considerably in the kinds of illness-related images they construct (Benoliel, 1974; Wortman and Dunkel-Schetter, 1979); and their images have considerable effect on those close to them (van den Berg, 1980). Reflection on one's own experience of illness may be helpful here. I remember, as a child, feeling strange and uncomfortable as I lay in bed, and wondering how ill I was. My answer came from how quiet the house was. If my parents were keeping it so quiet, then they must have been very worried about me! My parents' images, then, influenced my own image of my illness, and I came to worry more about myself. Sometimes a family can go so far as to define most of the images of their ill member, for example, in their anticipation of his death they can leave him very little opportunity for living (Le Shan, 1977). The influence of the image that Mollie's family had of her on her own self-image is a good example. In a different way, the images of Gordon's family influenced his illness-related images by keeping him isolated from them.

Some information is available about what kind of family can best cope with the illness of a member. It is a family which has a flexible set of images, the implications of which open doors rather than close them. Families which can change the way they organize themselves relatively easily, share the decision-making between all family members and allow its members a high degree of autonomy deal with it relatively well. These families have been described as energized families (Pratt, 1976). It follows that any procedure which frees up the images of a family so that they can function in this way will free up energy for the effective and empathic support of their ill or injured member (Viney, Benjamin and Preston, in pressb).

The illness-related images of health care professionals also vary as much as those of the people they treat (Blumberg, Flaherty and Lewis, 1980). There is, unfortunately, evidence that these images can have negative effects (Anderson, 1981; Plutchik et al., 1974; Taylor, 1979). There is also evidence that this influence can be turned to good effect (Hinton, 1980). The medical and nursing staff who changed their helplessness-laden images of people hospitalized with terminal cancer (Klagsbrun, 1970) and of elderly people in nursing homes (Langner and Rodin, 1976) to images of them as responsible decision-makers, and helped them to become such decision-makers, testify to this. There have also been examples cited in this book of health care professionals working with ill people to effect some change in their view of the world. Physicians helped Gordon's family to stop isolating him and Rachael to recapture her old image of competence. A physiotherapist helped the ill woman who could not believe that healthy people could empathize with her. It was a nurse who encouraged George to prepare, with more reality-based images, for his haemorrhoid surgery.

Health care professionals are human too. They are as vulnerable as most people to illness and death. They are therefore as vulnerable to illness-related images of uncertainty, anxiety and anger, helplessness, depression and isolation. Just as the ill and injured people they work with need to become aware of their own images and their role in creating and maintaining them so do physicians, other therapists and nurses. Only then can they learn to empathize accurately and communicate effectively with ill people and their families and friends.

Reflections

It is appropriate that the concluding comments in a book about images should concern reflections. Reflection implies a bending back on oneself, as one's images in a mirror is bent back. Technically, reflection can be said to represent the return of light or sound waves from a surface. A more general definition of reflection describes it as thoughts formed as a result of meditation.

All of these aspects of reflection are important to people who are ill. They can gain from reflecting on their own images and their role in developing them. This reflection can be carried out when alone, whether it be by meditation, dream analysis or careful observation of their own actions. It can also be done effectively with help from other people such as with health care professionals, counsellors, family members or in groups with other people who are ill. Health care professionals can also reflect profitably on the illness-related images of the people they work with, as well as on their own images of illness.

The notion of reflection is also relevant to the kind of research which has been reported here. By "bending back" reflectively on people's accounts of their illness, we have been able to identify patterns of images which were not clear before. It follows, too, that the images I have used in presenting this report are open to further

233

reflection. You, the reader, must now be the one to reflect.

REFERENCES

Abram, H.S. (1970). Survival by machine: The psychological stress of chronic haemodialysis. Psychiatry in Medicine, 1 , 37-51.

Abram, H.S. (1972). The psychology of chronic illness. Journal of Chronic Disease, 25 , 659-664.

Abrams, R.D. & Finesinger, J.E. (1953). Guilt reactions in patients with cancer. Cancer, 6, 317-322.

Adams, J.E. & Lindemann, E. (1974). Coping with long-term disability. In G.V. Coelho, D.A. Hamburg, & J.E. Adams, (eds.), Coping with adaptation. N.Y.: Basic Books, pp. 127-138.

Affleck, G., Pfeiffer, C., Tennen, H. & Fifield, J. (1987). Attributional processes in rheumatoid arthritis patients. Arthritis Rheumatics, 8, 927-31.

Affleck, G., Tennen, H., Pfeiffer, C., Fifield, J. (1987). Appraisals of control and predictability in adapting to a chronic disease. Journal of Personality and Social Psychology, 2, 273-9.

Affleck, G., Tennen, H., Croog, S. & Levine, S. (1987). Causal attribution, perceived benefits and workability after a heart attack: An eight year study. Journal of Consulting and Clinical Psychology, 55, 29-35.

Agnew, N.McK. & Pyke, S.W. (1969). The science game. Englewood Cliffs, N.J.: Prentice-Hall.

Albrecht, G.L. & Higgins, P.C. (1977). Rehabilitation success: The interrelationships of multiple criteria. Journal of Health and Social Behaviour, 18 , 36-45.

Alexander, F. & French, T.M. (1948). Studies in psychosomatic medicine . New York: Ronald.

Alonzo, A.A. (1984). An illness behaviour paradigm: A conceptual exploration of a situational-adaptation perspective. Social Science and Medicine, 5, 499-510.

Allport, G.W. (1955). Becoming . New Haven: Yale University Press.

Anderson, N.D. (1981). Exclusion: A study of depersonalization in health care. Journal of Humanistic Psychology , 21 , 67-78.

Andreasen, N.J.C. & Norris, A.S. (1972). Long term adjustment and adaptation mechanisms in severely burned adults. Journal of Nervous and Mental Disease, 154, 352-362.

Andreasen, N.J.C., Noyes, R. & Hartford, C.E. (1972). Factors influencing adjustment of burn patients during hospitalization. Psychosomatic Medicine, 34, 517-525.

Andrew, J.M. (1970). Recovery from surgery with and without preparatory instruction for three coping styles. Journal of Personality and Social Psychology, 15, 223-226.

Ansbacher, H.L. & Ansbacher, R. (eds.) (1956). The individual psychology of Alfred Adler. N.Y.: Basic Books.

Antaki, C. & Brewin, C. (eds.). (1982). Attributions and psychological change, New York: Academic Press.

Antonovsky, A. (1979). Health, stress and coping. San Francisco, California: Jossey Bass.

Armistead, N. (1974). Experience in every day life. In Armistead, N. (ed.). Reconstructing social psychology . London: Houghton Mifflin.

Arnkoff, D.B. (1986). A comparison of the aging and restructing components of cognitive restructing. Cognitive Therapy and Research, 10, 147-158.

Ashcroft, J.J., Leinster, S.J. & Slade, P.D. (1986). Mastectomy versus breast conservation: Psychological effects of patients' choice of treatment. In M. Watson & S. Greer (eds.) Psychosocial issues in malignant disease. Oxford: Pergamon.

Australian Bureau of Statistics. (1979). Australian health survey 1977-1978 . Canberra: Australian Government Printer.

Baider, L. & Sarell, M. (1983). Perceptions and causal attributions of Isreali women with breast cancer concerning their illness: The effects of ethnicity and religiosity. Psychotherapy and Psychosomatics, 3, 136-43.

Bakan, D. (1967). On method . San Francisco: Jossey Bass.

Bandura, A. (1984). Recycling misconceptions of perceived self efficacy. Cognitive Therapy and Research, 8, 231-255.

Bannister, D. Comment on Eysenck, H.J. (1970). Explanation and the concept of personality. In R.T. Borger, & F. Cioffi, (eds.), Explanation in the behavioural sciences. Cambridge: Cambridge University Press.

Bannister, D. & Fransella, F. (1980). Inquiring man. London: Penguin.

Bard, M. (1970). The price of survival for cancer victims. In Strauss, A.L. (ed.), When medicine fails. Chicago: Aldine.

Bard, M. & Sutherland, A.M. (1977). The psychological impact of cancer. New York: The American Cancer Society.

Bartop, R. N., Lazarus, L. & Luckhurst, E. et al., (1977). Depressed lymphocyte function after bereavement. Lancet, 2, 834-836.

Bassett, D.L. & Pilowsky, I. (1985). A study of brief psychotherapy for chronic pain. Journal of Psychosomatic Research, 3, 259-64.

Bazeley, P. & Viney, L.L. (1974). Women coping with crisis: A preliminary community study. Journal of Community Psychology, 2, 391-398.

Beck, A.T. (1967). Depression: Clinical, experimental and theoretical aspects. New York: Harper & Row.

Beck, A.T., Emery, G. & Greenberg, R.L. (1985). Anxiety disorders and phobias: A cognitive perspective. New York: Basic Books.

Beck, A.T., Rush, A. J., Shaw, B.F. & Emery, G. (1979). Cognitive therapy of depression. New York: Guilford.

Beloff, J. (1973). Psychological sciences: A review of modern psychology. London: Grosby Lockwood Staples.

Benoliel, J.Q. (1974). The dying patient and the family. In S.E. Troup, & W.A. Greene, (eds.), The patient, death and the family. New York: Scribners.

Benoliel, J.Q. (1985). Loss and terminal illness. Nursing Clinics of North America, 2, 439-48.

Ben-Sira, Z. (1984). Chronic illness and stress and coping. <u>Social Sciences and Medicine</u>, <u>4</u> 725-36.

Berger, P.L. & Luckman, T. (1972). <u>The social construction of reality</u>. London: Penguin.

Bernal, E.W. (1984). Immobility and the self: A clinical-existential inquiry. <u>Journal of Medical Philosophy</u>, <u>1</u>, 75-91.

Bhaskar, R. (1975). <u>A realist theory of science</u>. Leeds, England: Leeds Books.

Bishop, G.D. & Converse, S.A. (1986). Illness representations: A prototype approach. <u>Health Psychology</u>, <u>5</u>, 95-114.

Blacher, R.S. (1984). The briefest encounter: Psychotherapy for medical and surgical patients. <u>General Hospital Psychiatry</u>, <u>3</u>, 226-32.

Bloom, J.R. & Spiegel, D. (1984). The relationship of two dimensions of social support to the psychological well-being and social functioning of women with advanced breast cancer. <u>Social Sciences and Medicine</u>, <u>8</u>, 831-7.

Blumberg, B., Flaherty, M. & Lewis, J. (eds.) (1980). <u>Coping with cancer</u>. Washington, D.C.: U.S. Department of Health and Human Services.

Blumenthal, J.A., Thompson, L.W., Williams, R.B. & Kong, Y. (1979). Anxiety-proneness and coronary heart disease. <u>Journal of Psychosomatic Research</u>. <u>23</u>, 17-21.

Bogdan, R. & Taylor, S.J. (1975). Introduction to qualitative research

methods : A phenomenological approach to the social sciences.

N.Y.: Wiley.

Bonarius, H.C.J. (1970) Fixed role therapy: A double paradox. British

Journal of Medical Psychology, 43 , 213-219.

Boring, E.G. (1953). A history of introspection. Psychological Bulletin,

50. 169-189.

Boulding, K.W. (1956). The image: Knowledge in life and society.

Ann Arbor: The University of Michigan Press.

Bower, G.H. (1981). Mood and memory. American Psychologist , 36,

129-148.

Bowlby, J. (1961). Processes of mourning. The International Journal

of Psychoanalysis, 42 , 317-340.

Brentano, F. (1955). Psychologie vom empirischen standpunkt.

Hamburg: Meiner.

Brickman, P., Kidder, L.H., Coates, D. Rabinowitz, V., Cohn, G. &

Karuza, J. (1983). The dilemas of helping: Making aid fair and

effective. In J.D. Fisher, A. Nadler, & B.M. De Paulo, (eds.).

New directions in helping, Vol. 1 New York: Academic Press.

17-49.

Brickman, P., Rabinowitz, V., Karuza, J. Coates, D., Cohn, G. & Kidder,

L.H. (1982). Models of helping and coping. American

Psychologist, 37, 368-384.

Bridgman, P.W. (1959). The way things are. Cambridge, Mass.:

Harvard University Press.

Brody, H. (1987). Stories of sickness. New Haven: Yale.

Bronner-Huszar, J. (1971). The psychological aspects of cancer in man. Psychosomatics, 12, 133-138.

Brown, J. & Rawlinson, M. (1976). The morale of patients following open heart surgery. Journal of Health and Social Behaviour, 17, 134-144.

Bruner, J.S. (1962). On knowing: essays for the left hand. Cambridge: Harvard University Press,

Bruhn, J.G., Chandler, B. & Wolf, S. (1969). A psychological study of survivors and non-survivors of myocardial infarction. Psychosomatic Medicine, 31, 8-19.

Bryant, B.K. & Trockel, J.F. (1976). Personal history of psychological stress related to locus of control orientation among college women. Journal of Consulting and Clinical Psychology, 44, 226-271.

Bulman, R.J. & Wortman, C.B. (1977). Attribution of blame and coping in the 'real world': Severe accident victims react to their lot. Journal of Personality and Social Psychology 35, 351-363.

Bunn, T. A. & Clarke, A.M. (1979). Crisis intervention: An experimental study of the effects of a brief period of counselling on the anxiety of relations of seriously injured or ill hospital patients. British Journal of Medical Psychology, 5, 191-195.

Burish, T.G., Carey, M.P., Wallston, K.A., Stein, M.J., Jamison, R.N. & Lyles, J.N. (1984). Health locus of control and chronic disease: An external orientation may be advantegeous. Journal of Social and Clinical Psychology, 2, 326-332.

Byrne, D.G. & Whyte, H.M. (1978). Dimensions of illness behaviour in survivors of myocardial infarction. Journal of Psychosomatic Research, 22 , 485-491.

Byrne, D.G., Whyte, H.M. & Butler, K.L. (1981). Illness behaviour and outcome following survived myocardial infarction: A prospective study. Journal of Psychosomatic Research, 25 , 97-107.

Canter, A., Imboden, J.B., & Cluff, L.E. (1966). The frequency of physical illness as a function of prior psychological vulnerability and contemporary stress. Psychosomatic Medicine, 28, 344-350.

Cantor, R.C. (1986). Self-esteem, sexuality and cancer-related stress. In J.M. Vaeth (ed.) Body image, self-esteem and sexuality in cancer patients. San Francisco: Karger.

Caplan, G. (1964). Principles of preventative psychiatry. New York: Basic Books.

Carey, R.C. (1974). Emotional adjustment in terminal patients: A quantitative approach. Journal of Counselling Psychology, 21, 433-439.

Carlson, R. (1971). Sex differences in ego functioning: Exploratory studies of agency and communion. Journal of Consulting and Clinical Psychology , 37 , 267-277.

Carter, E.A. & Orfanidis, M.M. (1976). Family therapy with one person and the family therapist's own family. In P.J. Guerin, (ed.), Family therapy. New York: Gardner.

Casey, R.L., Masuda, M. & Holmes, T.M. (1967) Quantitative study of recall of life events. Journal of Psychosomatic Medicine, 11, 239-247.

Cassell, E.J. (1976a). The healer's art. Middlesex: Penguin.

Cassell, E.J. (1976b). The contribution of the social environment to host resistance. American Journal of Epidemiology, 104, 107-123.

Cassens, B.J. (1985). Social consequences of the Acquired Immune Deficiency Syndrome. Annals of Internal Medicine. 5, 768-71.

Chapman, C.R. & Cox, G.B. (1977). Anxiety, pain and depression surrounding elective surgery: A multivariate comparison of abdominal surgery patients with kidney donars and recipients. Journal of Psychosomatic Research, 21 7-15.

Chapman, S.L. & Brena, S.I. (1982). Learned helplessness and responses to nerve blocks in chronic low back pain patients. Pain, 14, 355-364.

Clarke, A.M. & Viney, L.L. (1979). The primary prevention of illness: A psychological perspective. Australian Psychologist, 4, 7-20.

Cleary, P.D., Mechnaic, D. & Greenley, J.R. (1982). Sex differences in medical care utilization: An empirical investigation. Journal of Health and Social Behaviour, 23, 106-118.

Cleghorn, J.M. & Streiner, B.J. (1979). Prediction of symptoms and illness behaviour from measures of life change and verbalized depressive themes. Journal of Human Stress , 5 , 16-23.

Cohen, F. & Lazarus, R.S. (1973) Active coping processes, coping dispositions and recovery from surgery. Psychosomatic Medicine , 35 , 375-389.

Cohen, F. & Lazarus, R.S. (1979). Coping with the stresses of illness. In G.C. Stone, F. Cohen & N.E. Adler, (eds.), Health Psychology - A Handbook. San Francisco: Jossey Bass.

Congalton, A.A. (1969). Status and prestige in Australia. Melbourne: Cheshire.

Coser, R.L. (1959). Some social functions of laughter: A study of humour in a hospital setting. Human Relations , 12 , 171-182.

Cousins, N. (1979). Anatomy of an illness (as perceived by the patient). In C. Garfield, (ed.), Stress and survival . St. Louis: Mosby.

Cowie, B. (1976). The cardiac patient's perception of his heart attack. Social Science and Medicine , 10 , 87-96.

Craig, T.J. & Abeloff, M.D. (1974). Psychiatric symptomatology among hospitalized cancer patients. The American Journal of Psychiatry, 131, 1323-1327.

Croog, S.H., Shapiro, D.S. & Levine, S. (1971). Denial among heart patients. Psychosomatic Medicine , 33 , 385-389.

Cummings, N.A. & Vandenbos, G.R. (1979). The general practice of psychology. Professional Psychology , 10 , 431-440.

Cummings, S.T., Godfrey, A.E. & Burrows, B. (1969). Personality and social class factors associated with occupational disability in patients with chronic obstructive lung disease. American Review of Personality Disease, 99 , 872-878.

D'Afflitti, J.G. & Weitz, G.W. (1974). Rehabilitating the stroke patient through patient-family groups. International Journal of Group Psychotherapy, 25 , 323-332.

de Beauvoir, S. (1973). A very easy death. New York: Warner.

Dean, K. (1986). Lay care in illness. Social Science and Medicine, 2, 275-84.

Dellipiani, A.W., Cay, E.L., Philip, A.E., Vetter, N.J., Colling, W.A., Donaldson, R.J. & McCormack, P. (1976). Anxiety after a heart attack. British Heart Journal, 38 , 752-757.

Dembroski, T.M., Weiss, S.M., Shields, J.L., Haynes, S.G. & Feinleib, M. (eds.) (1978). Coronary-prone behaviour. N.Y.: Springer-Verlag.

Derogatis, L.R. (1986). The Psychosocial Adjustment to Illness Scale (PAIS). Journal of Psychosomatic Research, 30, 77-91.

Derogatis, L.R., Abeloff, M.D. & Melisaratos, N. (1979). Psychological coping mechanisms and survival time in metastatic breast cancer. Journal of the American Medical Association, 242, 1504-1508.

Doehrman, S.R. (1977). Psychosocial aspects of recovery from coronary heart disease: A review. Social Science and Medicine, 11, 199-218.

Dilley, J.N., Cohitill, H.N. & Perl, M. et.al, (1985). Findings in psychiatric consultations with patients with Acquired Immune Deficiency Syndrome. American Journal of Psychiatry, 142, 82-86.

Dollard, J., Miller, N.E., Doob, C.W., Mowrer, O. & Sears, R.R. (1939). Frustration and aggression. New Haven: Yale University Press.

Dorossiev, D., Paskova, V. & Zachariev, Z. (1976). Psychological problems of cardiac rehabilitation. In V. Stocksmeier, (ed.), Psychological approaches to the rehabilitation of coronary patients . New York: Springer Verlag.

Duval, M.L. (1984). Psychosocial metaphors of physical distress among MS patients. Social Science and Medicine, 6, 635-8.

Early, G.L. & Redfearing, D.L. (1979). Anxiety in ambulatory emergency patients. Journal of the American College of Physicians, 8 , 350-352.

Egger, J., & Stix, P. (1984). The coping process with illness in patients with cardiovascular or cerebrovascular diseases : A new survey: International Journal of Rehabilitation Research, 2, 135-42.

Eil, K.O. (1985). Coping with serious illness: On intergrating constructs to enhance clinical research, assessment and intervention. International Journal of Psychiatry in Medicine, 4, 335-56.

Ellis, A. (1984). The essence of R.E.T. - 1984. Journal of Rational - Emotive Therapy, 2, 19-26.

Engelmann, M.W. (1976). The diabetic client. In Turner, F.J. (ed.), Differential diagnosis and treatment in social work. New York: Free press.

Epting, F.R. (1984). Personal construct counselling and psychotherapy, New York: Wiley.

Epting, F.R. & Neimeyer, R.A. (Eds.). Personal meanings of death. New York: Hemisphere.

Epting, F.R. & Nazario, A. (1987). Designing a fixed role therapy: Issues, techniques and modifications. In R.A. Niemeyer & G.J. Neimeyer (eds.) A casebook in personal construct therapy. New York: Springer.

Evans, D.A., Bloer, H.R., Steinberg, G.R. & Penrose, A.M. (1986). Frames and heuristics in doctor-patient discourse. Social Science and Medicine, 22, 1027-1034.

Farber, I.J. (1978). Hospitalized cardiac patients: Some psychological aspects. New York State Journal of Medicine, Nov., 2045-2049.

Farrelly, F. & Brandsma, J. (1974). Provocative therapy. Port Collins, Colorado: Sheilds.

Faulstich, M.E. (1987). Psychiatric aspects of AIDS. American Journal of Psychiatry, 144, 551-556.

Fava, G.A., Zielezny, M. Pilowsky, I. & Trombini, G. (1984). Patterns of depression and illness behaviour in general hospital patients. Psychopathology, 3, 105-9.

Feigenberg, L. & Shneidman, E.S. (1979). Clinical thanatology and psychotherapy: Some reflections on caring for the dying person. Omega , 10 , 1-8.

Feldman, D.A. & Johnston, T.M. (eds.) (1986). The social context of an epidemic, New York: Roeger.

Felton, B.J. & Revenson, T.A. (1984). Coping with chronic illness: A study of illness controllability and the influence of coping strategies on psychological adjustment. Journal of Consulting and Clinical Psychology, 3, 343-53.

Firth-Cozens, J. & Brewin, C.R. (in press). Attributional change during psychotherapy. British Journal of Clinical Psychology.

Fischer, C.T. (1985). Individualising psychological assessment. Monterey, California: Brooks Cole.

Fischer, W.F. (1974). On the phenomenological mode of research "being anxious." Journal of Phenomenological Psychology, 4, 405-423.

Forester, B., Kornfeld, D.S. & Fleiss, J. (1982). Effects of psychotherapy on patient distress during radiotherapy for cancer. Psychosomatic Medicine, 44, 118-126.

Forsyth, G.L., Delaney, K.D. & Gresham, M.L. (1984). Vying for a winning position: Management style of the chronically ill. Research in Nursing & Health , 3, 181-8.

Fransella, F. (1985). Individual psychotherapy. In E. Button (ed.) Personal construct theory and mental health. Beckenham: Croom Helm.

Fransella, F. (1987). Stuttering to fluency via reconstruing. In R.A. & G. J. Neimeyer (eds.) Personal construct therapy casebook. New York: Springer.

Freud, S. (1928). Humour. Collected papers (Vol. 5). London: Hogarth, 1950

Friedman, H.S. & Di Matteo, M.R. (1979). Health care as an interpersonal process. Journal of Social Issues , 35 , 1-11.

Friedman, M. & Rosenman, R.H. (1974). Type A behaviour and your heart . New York: Knopf.

Galton, F. (1889). Natural inheritance . London: A.M.S. Press.

Gannick, D. & Jesperson, M. (1984). Lay concepts and strategies for handling symptoms of disease. Scandivanian Journal of Primary Health Care, 2, 67-76.

Garron, D.C. & Leavitt, F. (1983). Chronic low back pain and depression. Journal of Clinical Psychology, 4, 486-93.

Gartner, A. & Riessman, F. (1977). Self-help in the human services . San Francisco: Jossey Bass.

Gendlin, E.T. (1962). Experiencing and the creation of meaning. N.Y.: Free Press of Glencoe.

Gendlin, E.T. (1973). Experiential psychotherapy. In Corsini, R. (ed.), Current psychotherapies . Illinois: Peacock.

Gendlin, E.T. (1981). Focusing . New York: Bantum.

Gendlin, E.T. (1985). Let your body interpret your dreams. Wilmette, Illinois: Chiron.

Gergen, K.J. (1985). The social construtionist movement in modern psychology. American Psychologist, 40, 266-275.

Giddens, A. (1976). New rules of sociological method London: Hutchinson.

Giorgi, A. (1971). The experience of the subject as a source of data in a psychological experiment. In A. Giorgi, W.F. Fischer, & R. Von Eckartsberg, (eds.), Duquesne studies in phenomenological psychology . Pittsburgh, Pennsylvania.: Duquesne University Press, No. 1.

Giorgi, A. (ed.) (1985). Phenomenology and social psychological research. Pittsburgh, Pennsylvania: Duquesne University.

Giorgi, A. , Barton, A. & Maes, C. (eds.) (1983). Duquesne Studies in Phenomenological Psychology. 4, Pittsburgh, Pennsylvania: Duquesne University.

Girodo, M. (1977). Self talk: Mechanisms in anxiety and stress management. In C. Speilberger, & Z. Sarason, (eds.), Stress and anxiety , Vol. 4. Washington, D.C.: Hemisphere.

Glaser, B. & Straus, A. (1968). Time for dying . Chicago: Aldine.

Glaser, B. & Straus, A. (1967). The discovery of grounded theory: Strategies for qualitative research, Chicago: Aldine Atherton.

Gleser, G.C. & Ihilevich, D. (1969) A projective instrument for defense mechanisms. Journal of Counselling and Clinical Psychology , 33, 51-60.

Glidewell, J.C. (1972). A social psychology of mental health. In S.E. Golann, & C. Eisdorfer, (eds.), Handbook of community mental health. N.Y.: Appleton-Century-Crofts, 211-246.

Golan, N. (1978). Treatment in crisis situations. New York: Free Press.

Goldberg, J.C. (Ed.) (1982). Psychotherapeutic treatment of cancer patients. New York: Free Press.

Gordon, D. (1978). Therapeutic metaphors. Cupertino, California: Meta.

Gordon, R. (1972). A very private world. In P. Sheehan, (ed.), The function and nature of imagery. New York: Academic Press.

Gottesman, D. & Lewis, M.S. (1982). Differences in crisis reactions among cancer and surgery patients. Journal of Consulting and Clinical Psychology, 50, 381-388.

Gottlieb, B.H. (1985). Social networks and social support: An overview of research, practice and policy implications. Health Education Quarterly, 1, 5-22.

Gottschalk, L.A. (1985). How to understand and analyse your own dreams. California: Art Reproduction Press.

Gottschalk, L.A. (1978) Psychosomatic medicine today: An overview. Psychosomatics, 19, 89-93.

Gottschalk, L.A. (1979). The content analysis of verbal behaviour: Further studies. New York: SP Medical & Scientific Books.

Gottschalk, L.A. & Gleser, G.C. (1969.) The measurement of psychological states from the content analysis of verbal behaviour . Berkeley: University of California Press.

Gottschalk, L.A. & Hoigaard, J. (1986). Emotional impact of mastechomy. In L.A. Gottschalk, F. Lolas & L.L. Viney (eds.) Content analysis of verbal behaviour: Significance in clinical medicine and psychiatry, Heidelberg: Springer Verlag.

Gottschalk, L.A., Lolas F. & Viney, L. L. (eds.) (1986). Content analysis of verbal behaviour in clinical medicine. Heidelberg: Springer.

Gottschalk, L.A., Winget, C.N. & Gleser, G.C. (1969). Manual of instructions for using the Gottschalk-Gleser content analysis scales . Berkeley: University of California Press.

Greenberger, E. & Sorensen, A.B. (1974). Toward a concept of psychosocial maturity. Journal of Youth and Adolescence , 3 , 329-358.

Greer, S. (1985). Cancer: Psychiatric aspects In K. Granville, & G.R. Ussman, (eds.) Recent advances in clinical psychology. Edinburgh: Churchill Livingstone.

Greer, S. (1987). Psychotherapy for the cancer patient. Psychiatric Medicine, 5, 267-279.

Greer, S. & Moorey, S. (1987). Advanced psychological therapy for patients with cancer. European Journal of Surgical Oncology, 13, 511-516.

Greer, S. & Morris, T. (1974). Psychological attributes of women who develop breast cancer. Journal of Psychosomatic Research , 19, 147-153.

Greer, S., Morris, T. & Pettingale, K.W. (1982). Psychological response to breast cancer: Effect on outcome. Lancet, 111, 785-787.

Greer, S. & Watson, M. (1987). Mental adjustment to cancer: Its measurement and prognostic importance. Cancer Surveys, 6, 439-453.

Grieger, R.M. (1985). The process of rational-emotive therapy. Journal of Rational-Emotive Therapy, 3, 138-148.

Gruen, W. (1975). Effects of brief psychotherapy during the hospitalization period on recovery processes in heart attacks. Journal of Consulting and Clinical Psychology , 43 , 223-232.

Gruner, C.R. (1978). Understanding laughter . Chicago: Nelson Hall.

Guerney, B.G. (1977). Relationship enhancement . San Francisco: Jossey Bass.

Gunderson, E.K.E. & Rahe, R.H. (eds.) (1974). Life stress and illness . Springfield, Ill.: Thomas.

Haan, N. (1977). Coping and defending . New York: Academic Press.

Hackett, T.P. & Cassem, N.H. (1975) . Psychological management of the myocardiac infarction patient. Journal of Human Stress , 6 , 69-101.

Hackett, T.P., Cassem, N.H. & Wishnie, H.A. (1968). The coronary care unit: An appraisal of its psychologic hazards. New England Journal of Medicine, 279, Pt. 25, 1365-1370.

Hamburg, D.A. (1974) . Coping behaviour in life threatening circumstances. Psychotherapy and Psychosomatics , 23 , 13-25.

Hamera, E.K. & Shontz, F.C. (1978). Perceived positive and negative effects of life threatening illness. Journal of Psychosomatic Research, 22, 419-424.

Harré, R. (1974). Blueprint for a new science. In N. Armistead, (ed.) Reconstructing social psychology . Middlesex: Penguin.

Harré, R. & Secord, P.T. (1972). The explanation of social behaviour . Oxford: Blackwell.

Hartsfield, J. & Clopton, J.R. (1985). Reducing presurgical anxiety: A possible visitor effect. Social Science and Medicine, 5, 529-33.

Harvey, J.H. & Weary, G. (1985). Attribution: Basic issues and applications. Orlando, Florida: Academic Press.

Haynes, S.G., Levine, S., Scotch, N., Feinlab, M. & Kannel, W.B. (1978). The relationship of psychosocial factors to coronary heart disease in the Framingham study. American Journal of Epidemiology, 107 , 362-383.

Heffernon, E.W. & Lippincott, R.C. (1966). The gastrointestinal response to stress (the irritable colon). Medical Clinics of North America , 50 , 591-595.

Henrichs, T.F., Mackenkie, J.W. & Almond, C.H. (1969). Psychological adjustment and acute response to open heart surgery. Journal of Nervous and Mental Disease , 148 , 158-164.

Hetherington, R. (1983). Sacred cows and white elephants. Bulletin of the British Psychological Society, 36, 273-280.

Hlatky, M.A., Haney, T., Barefoot, J.C., Califf, R.M., Mark, D.B., Pryor, D.B. & Williams, R.B. (1986). Medical, psychological and social correlates of work disability among men with coronary artery disease. American Journal of Cardiology, 10, 911-5.

Hinkle, L.E. (1974). The effect of exposure to culture change, social change, and changes in interpersonal relationships on health. In B.S. & B.P. Dohrenwend, (eds.), Stressful life events: Their nature and effects . New York: Wiley.

Hinton, J. (1980). The cancer ward. Advances in Psychosomatic Medicine , 10 , 78-98.

Hobfoll, S.F. & Walfisch, S. (1984). Coping with a threat to life: A longitudinal study of self, concept, social support and psychological distress. American Journal of Community Psychology, 12, 87-100.

Hobson, R.F. (1985). Forms of feeling. London: Tavistock.

Holland, J.C. & Tross, S. (1985). The psychosocial and neuropsychiatric sequelae of the immuno-deficiency syndrome and related disorders. Annals of Internal Medicine, 103, 760-764.

Holland, J.C., Rowland, J., Lebovits, A. & Rusalen, R. (1979). Reactions to cancer treatment. Psychiatric Clinics of North America , 2 , 347-358.

Holland, R. (1970). George Kelly: Constructive innocent and reluctant existensialist. In D. Bannister, (ed.), Perspectives in personal construct theory . London: Academic Press.

Hudson, L. (1972). The cult of the fact . London: Jonathon Cape.

Hughson, A.V., Cooper, A.F., McArdle, C.S. & Smith, D.C. (1986). Psychological impact of adjuvant chemotherapy in the first two years after mastectomy. British Medical Journal, 87, 1268-1271.

Hurst, M.W., Jenkins, C.D. & Rose, R.M. (1976). The relation of psychological stress to onset of medical illness. Annual Review of Medicine, 27, 301-312.

Hurvitz, N. (1974). Peer self-help psychotherapy groups: Psychotherapy without psychotherapists. In Trice, R.B. (ed.), The sociology of psychotherapy . New York: Aronson.

Husserl, E. (1927). Phenomenology. Encyclopaedia Britannia, 14 (17), 699-702.

Hutschnecker, A.A. (1981). Hope . New York: Putnam.

Ilfield, F.W. (1980). Coping styles of Chicago adults: Description. Journal of Human Stress, 6, 2-10.

Irwin, M., Daniels, M. & Weiner, H. (1987). Immune and neuroendocrine changes during bereavement. Psychiatric Clinics of North America, 10, 449-465.

Jamison, K.R., Wellisch, D.K. & Pasnau, R.O. (1978). Psychosocial aspects of mastectomy: The woman's perspective. American Journal of Psychiatry, 133, 432-436.

Janis, I.L. & Mann, L. (1977). Decision-making: A psychological analysis of conflict, chance and commitment . New York: Free Press.

Janis, I.L. & Rodin, J. (1979). Attribution, control and decision-making: Social psychology and health. In G.C. Stone, F. Cohen, & N.E. Adler, (eds.), Health Psychology - A Handbook . San Francisco: Jossey-Bass.

Jasnow, A. (1981). Humour and survival. Voices , 16 , 50-54.

Jessop, D.J. & Stein, R.E. (1985). Uncertainty and its relation to the psychological and social correlates of chronic illness in children. Social Science, 10, 993-9.

Johnson, J.E. & Leventhal, H. (1974). Effects of accurate expectations and behavioural instructions on reactions during a noxious medical examination. Journal of Personality and Social Psychology , 29 , 710-718.

Johnson, J.H. & Sarason, I.G. (1978). Life stress, depression and anxiety: Internal-external control as a moderator variable. Journal of Psychosomatic Research, 22 , 205-208.

Johnson, M. & Carpenter, L. (1980). Pre-operative anxiety. Psychological Medicine, 10, 361-367.

Jones, E.E. & Davis, K.E. (1965). From acts to dispositions. In L.

   Berkowitz. (ed.), Advances in experimental social psychology,

   Vol. 2. N.Y.: Academic Press.

Jung, C.G. (1968). The archetypes and the collective unconscious.

   Collected Works , (Vol. 9). Princeton: Princeton University

   Press, (1934).

Kane, T.R., Suls, J. & Tedeschi, J.T. (1977). Humour as a tool of social

   interaction. In A.J. Chapman, & H.C. Foot, (eds.), Its a funny

   thing, humour. Oxford: Pergamon.

Kant, I. (1934). Critique of pure reason . London: Macmillan.

Kanter, R.M. (1975). Women and the structure of organizations. In M.

   Milman, & R.M. Kanter, (eds.), Another voice . New York:

   Anchor.

Kaplan, B.H., Cassel, J.C. & Gore, S. (1977). Social support and

   health. Medical Care, 15 , 47-58.

Karst, T.O. & Trexler, L.D. (1970). Initial study using fixed role and

   rational-emotive therapy in treating public speaking anxiety.

   Journal of Consulting and Clinical Psychology, 34, 360.

Kasanen, A. & Forsstrom, J. (1966). Social stress and living habits in

   the etiology of peptic ulcer. Annual Medical International Forum,

   55, 13-22.

Katz, J.L., Weiner, H., Gallagher, T.F. & Hellman, L. (1970). Stress and

   ego defenses: Psychoendocrine response to impending breast

   tumor biopsy. Archives of General Psychiatry 23, 131-142.

Keefe, F.J. & Dolan, G. (1986). Pain behaviour and pain coping strategies in lower back pain and myofacial pain dysfunction syndrome patients. Pain, 24, 49-156.

Keefe, F.J., Wilkins, R.H., Cook, W.A. Jr., Crisson, J.E. & Muhlbaier, L.H. (1986). Depression, pain and pain behaviour. Journal of Consulting and Clinical Psychology, 5, 665-9.

Keen, E. (1975). A primer in phenomenological psychology. N.Y.: Holt, Rinehart & Winston.

Keen, E. (1977). Existensial-phenomenological therapy. In Rimm, D. & Somervill, J.W. (eds.), Abnormal psychology. New York: Academic Press.

Kelly, G.A. (1955). The psychology of personal constructs. New York: Norton, Vols. 1 & 2.

Kelly, G.A. (1964). The language of hypothesis: Man's psychological instrument. Journal of Industrial Psychology, 20, 137-152.

Kelly, G.A. (1965). The strategy of psychological research. Bulletin of the British Psychological Society, 18, 1-15.

Kelly, G.A. (1969a). Epilogue: Don Juan. In Maher, B. (ed.), Clinical psychology and personality. New York: Wiley.

Kelly, G.A. (1969b). Ontological acceleration. In Maher, B. (ed.), Clinical psychology and personality. New York: Wiley.

Kelly, G.A. (1970). A brief introduction to personal construct theory. In D. Bannister, (ed.), Perspectives in personal construct theory. New York: Academic Press.

Kelly, M.P. (1986). The subjective experience of chronic disease: Some implications for the management of ulcerative colitis. Journal of Chronic Diseases, 8. 23-34.

Keltikangas-Jlarvinen, L. (1986). Psychological meaning of illness and coping with disease. Psychotherapy and Psychosomatics, 2, 85-90.

Kempler, W. (1973). Gestalt therapy. In Corsini, R. (ed.), Current psychotherapies. Illinois: Peacock.

Kessler, R.C. (1979). Stress, social status and psychological distress. Journal of Health and Social Behaviour, 26, 259-272.

Khatami, M. & Rush, A.J. (1982). A one year follow-up of the multi-model treatment for current pain. Pain, 14, 45-52.

Kiecolt-Glaser, J.K. & Williams, D.A. (1987). Self-blame compliance and distress among burn patients. Journal of Personality and Social Psychology, 1, 187-93.

Kimball, C.P. (1980). Liaison psychiatry: The extension of a concept. Psychosomatics, 21, 684-687.

Kinsman, R.A., Jones, N.F., Matus, I. & Schum, R.A. (1976). A scale for measuring attitudes towards respiratory illness and hospitalization. Journal of Nervous and Mental Disorders, 163, 160-165.

Klagsbrun, S.C. (1970). Cancer, emotions and nurses. American Journal of Psychiatry 126 , 1237-1244.

Kleinman, A. (1986). Some uses and misuses of social science in medicine. In D.W. Fiske & R.A. Shweder (eds.) Metatheory in social science. Chicago: University of Chicago Press.

Kockelmans, J.J. (1966). Phenomenology and physical science. Pittsburgh, Pa.: Duquesne University Press.

Koestler, A. (1964). The act of creation. New York: Pantheon.

Kohler, N. (1938). The place of value in the world of facts. New York: Wiley.

Kornfeld, D.S. (1972). The hospital environment: Its impact on the patient. Advances in Psychosomatic Medicine, 8, 252-270.

Koslowsky, M., Kroog, S.H., La Voie, L. (1978). Perception of the etiology of illness: Causal attributions in a heart patient population. Perceptual and Motor Skills, 47, 475-485.

Kubler-Ross, E. (1969). On death and dying. New York: Macmillan.

Kuhlman, T.L. (1984). Humour and psychotherapy, Homewood: Illinois.

Landfield, A.W. (1965). Meaningfulness of self, ideal and other as related to own versus therapist's personal construct dimensions. Psychological Reports, 16, 605-608.

Landfield, A.W. & Epting, F.R. (1987). Personal construct psychology: Clinical and personality assessment, New York: Human Sciences.

Langer, E.J. & Rodin, J. (1976). The effects of choice and enhanced personal responsibility for the aged: A field experiment in an institutional setting. Journal of Personality and Social Psychology, 34, 191-198.

Langner, E.J., Janis, D.L. & Wolfer, J.A. (1975). Reduction of psychological stress in surgical patients. Journal of Experimental and Social Psychology, 11, 155-165.

Latour, B. & Woolgar, S. (1979). Laboratory life: The social construction of scientific facts, Beverley Hills: Sage.

Layden, M.A. (1982). Attribution style therapy. In C. Antaki & C. Brewin (eds.). Attributions and psychological change, New York: Academic Press.

LeShan, L. (1977). You can fight for your life. New York: Evans.

Leventhal, H., Meyer, D. & Nerenz, D. (1980). The common sense representation of illness changes. In S. Rachman (ed.) Medical psychology, New York: Pergamon.

Leventhal, H., Nerenz, D.R. & Steele, D.J. (1982). Illness representations and coping with health threats. In A. Baum & J. Singer (eds.) A handbook of psychology and health, Hillsdale, New Jersey: Lawrence Erlbaum.

Levine, J. (1977). Humour as a form of therapy. In A.J. Chapman, & H.C. Foot, (eds.), It's a funny thing, humour. Oxford: Pergamon.

Levitt, E.E. (1967). The psychology of anxiety. New York: Bobbs Merrill.

Lewis, F.M. & Bloom, J.R. (1978-79). Psychosocial adjustment to breast cancer: A review of selected literature. International Journal of Psychiatry in Medicine, 9, 1-17.

Lieber, L., Plumb, M.M., Gerstenzang, M.E. & Holland, J. (1976). The communication of affection between cancer patients and their spouses. Psychosomatic Medicine, 38, 379-389.

Lin, N., Simeone, R.S., Ensel, W.M. & Kuo, N. (1979). Social support, stressful life events and illness: A model and empirical test. Journal of Health and Social Behaviour, 20, 259-272.

Linden, M. (1985). Illness concepts of patients. Psychiatric Praxis, 1, 8-12.

Linn, J.G. & Husaini, B.A. (1985). Chronic medical problems, coping resources, and depression: A longitudinal study of rural Tennesseans. American Journal of Community Psychology, 6, 733-42.

Lipowski, Z.J. (1967). Review of consultation psychiatry and psychosomatic medicine. Psychosomatic Medicine, 29, 201-225.

Lipowski, Z.J., Lipsitt, D.R. & Whybrow, P.C. (eds.) (1977). Psychosomatic medicine. New York: Oxford University Press.

Litt, M.D. (1988). Self-efficacy and perceived control: Cognitive mediators of pain tolerance. Journal of Personality and Social Psychology, 54, 149-160.

LLoyd, J. & Laurence, K.M. (1985). Sequelae and support after termination of pregnancy for foetal malformation. British Medical Journal, 907-9.

Lofland, L.H. (1978). The craft of dying. Beverly Hills: Sage.

Luborsky, L. & McClellan, A.T. (1980-81). A sound mind in a sound body: To what extent do they go together before and after psychotherapy? International Journal of Psychiatry in Medicine, 10, 123-134.

Luborsky, L., Todd, T.C. & Katcher, A.H. (1973). A self-administered social assets scale for predicting physical and psychological illness and health. Journal of Psychosomatic Research, 17, 109-120.

Lucente, F.E. & Fleck, S. (1972). A study of hospitalization anxiety in 408 medical and surgical patients. Psychosomatic Medicine, 34, 304-312.

Lynch, J.J. (1977). The broken heart. New York: Harper & Row.

McCoy, M. (1977). Reconstruction of emotion. In D. Bannister, (ed.), New perspectives in personal construct theory. New York: Academic Press.

McCoy, M. (1980). Positive and negative emotion: A personal construct theory integration. In H. Bonarius, R. Holland, & S. Rosenberg, (eds.), Recent advances in the theory and practice of personal construct psychology. London: Macmillan.

McFarlane, A.H., Norman, G.R., Streiner, D.L. & Roy, R.G. (1984). Characteristics and correlates of effective and ineffective social supports. Journal of Psychosomatic Research, 6, 501-10.

McIvor, G.P., Riklan, M. & Reznikoff, M. (1984). Depression in multiple sclerosis as a function of length and severity of illness, age, remissions, and perceived social support. Journal of Clinical Psychology, 4, 1028-33.

McKay, D.A., Blake, R.L. Jr., Colwill, J.M., Brent, E.E., McCauley, J., Umlauf, F., Steakman, G.W. & Kivlahan, D. (1985). Social supports and stress as predictors of illness. Journal of Family Practice, 6, 575-81.

McKellar, P. (1962). The method of introspection. In J. Scher, (ed.), Theories of mind. New York: Free Press of Glencoe.

Mages, N.L. & Mendelsohn, G.A. (1979). Effects of cancer on patients' lives: A personalogical approach. In G.C.Stone, F. Cohen, & N.E. Adler, (eds.), Health Psychology . San Francisco: Jossey Bass.

Maguire, G.P., Lee, E.G., Bevington, D.J., Kuchemann, C.S., Crabtree, R.J. & Cornell, C.E. (1978). Psychiatric problems in the first year after mastectomy. British Medical Journal, 1, 963-965.

Mahrer, A.R. (1971). Personal life change through the systematic use of dreams. Psychotherapy: Theory, Research and Practice, 8, 828-832.

Mahrer, A.R. (1979). An invitation to theoreticians and researchers from an applied experiential practitioner. Psychotherapy: Theory, Research and Practice 16, 409-418.

Mahrer, A.R. (1980a). The treatment of cancer through experiential psychotherapy. Psychotherapy: Theory, Research and Practice, 17, 335-342.

Mahrer, A.R. (1980b). Research on theoretical concepts of psychotherapy. In W. Di Moor, & H.R. Wijngaarden, (eds.), Psychotherapy: Research, and Training. North Holland: Elsevier.

Mahrer, A.R. (1983). Experiential psychotherapy: Basic practices . New York: Bruner/Mazel.

Mair, J.M.M. (1970). Psychologists are human too. In Bannister, D. (ed.), Perspectives in personal construct theory. London: Academic Press.

Mair, J.M.M. (1976). Metaphors for living. Nebraska Symposium on Motivation, 24, 243-290.

Mancuso, J.C. (1979). Counselling from a personal construct perspective. International Journal for the Advancement of Counselling, 10, 305-313.

Manicas, P.T. & Secord, P.F. (1982). Implications for psychology from the new philosophy of science. American Psychologist, 38, 399-414.

Manne, S. & Sandler, I. (1984). Coping and adjustment to genital herpes. Journal of Behavioural Medicine, 7, 391-410.

Marias, J. (1967). Philosophical truth and the metaphoric system. In S.R. Hopper, & D.L. Miller, (eds.), Interpretation: The poetry of meaning. New York: Harbinger.

Marks, G., Richardson, J.L., Graham J.W. & Levine, A. (1986). Role of health locus of control beliefs and expectations of treatment efficacy in adjustment to cancer. Journal of Personality and Social Psychology, 2, 443-50.

Maslow, A.H. (1956). Philosophy of psychology. In J. Fairchild, (ed.), Personal problems and psychological frontiers. New York: Sheridan.

Mason, C. (1985). The production and effects of uncertainty with special references to diabetes mellitus. Social Science and Medicine, 12, 1329-34.

Matheny, K.B. & Cupp, P. (1983). Control, desirability, and anticipation as moderating variables between life change and illness. Journal of Human Stress, 2, 14-23.

Mechanic, D. (1974). Discussion of research programs on relations between stressful life events and episodes of physical illness. In B.S. & B.D. Dohrenwend, (eds.), Stressful life events: Their nature and effects. New York: Wiley.

Mechanic, D. (1977). Illness behaviour, social adaptation and the management of illness. Journal of Nervous and Mental Disorders, 165, 79-85.

Mechanic, D. (1978). Effects of psychological stress on perceptions of physical health and use of medical and psychiatric facilities. Journal of Human Stress, 4, 26-32.

Meichenbaum, D. (1977). Cognitive-behaviour modification: An integrative approach . New York: Plenum Press.

Melzak, R. (1980). Psychologic aspects of pain. In Bonica, J.J. (ed.), Pain . New York: Raven.

Menninger, K. (1959). Hope . Lecture given at the 115th Annual Meeting of the American Psychiatric Association, Philadelphia, Pennsylvania.

Meyer, R.G. & Haggerty, R.G. (1962). Streptococcal infections in families. Paediatrics, 29, 539-541.

Mickel, C. (1982). Innovative projects earning psychologists spots on hospital health care teams. American Psychologist, 37, 1350-1354.

Miller, D. (1986). Psychology, AIDS, ARC and PGL. In D. Miller (ed.) the management of AIDS patients Hampshire: Macmillan.

Miller, D. (1987). Living with AIDS and HIV. London: Macmillan.

Miller, D. & Brown, B. (1988). Developing the role of clinical psychology in the context of AIDS. The Psychologist, 2, 63-69.

Miller, W.B. (1978). Psychiatry and physical illness: The psychosomatic interface. In C.P. Rosenbaum, & J.E. Beebe, (eds.), Psychiatric treatment: crisis/clinic/consultation. New York: McGraw-Hill.

Mills, W.W. & Farrow, J.T. (1981). The transcendental meditation technique and acute experimental pain. Psychosomatic Medicine, 43, 157-164.

Millstein, S.G. & Irwin, C.E. (1987). Concepts of health and illness: Different constructs or variations on a theme? Health Psychology, 6, 515-524.

Mitchell, G.N. & Glicksman, A.S. (1977). Cancer patients: Knowledge and attitudes. Cancer, 4, 61-66.

Mitchell, K.R. & White, R.F. (1977). Behavioural self-management: An application to the study of migraine headaches. Behaviour Therapy, 8, 213-222.

Mlohlen, K. & Brahler, E. (1984). Complaint picture and self concept of patients with duodenal ulcer before and four years after surgery. Zeitschrift fur Psychosomatisch Medicin Psychoanalytisch, 30, 150-163.

Moorey, S. & Greer, S. (1987). Adjuvant psychological therapy: A manual for the treatment of patients with cancer. London: Cancer Research Campaign Psychological Medicine Group.

Moos, R.H. & Tsu, V.D. (1977). The crisis of physical illness: An overview. In R.H. Moos, (ed.), Coping with physical illness. New York: Plenum.

Moulton, J.M., Sweet, D.M. , Temoshok, L. & Mandel, L.S. (1987). Attributions of blame and responsibility in relation to distress and healthy behaviour change in people with AIDS and AIDS-related complex. Journal of Applied Social Psychology, 17, 493-506.

Namir, S., Wolcott, D.L., Fawzy, F.I. & Alumbaugh, M.J. (1987). Coping with AIDS: Psychological and coping implications. Journal of Applied Social Psychology, 17, 309-328.

Narboe, N. (1981). Why did the therapist cross the road? Voices, 16, 55-58.

Neimeyer, G.J. (1987). Personal construct assessment, strategy and technique. In R.A. & G.J. Neimeyer, (eds). Personal construct therapy casebook. New York: Springer.

Neimeyer, R.A.. (1985). Personal constructs in clinical practice. In P.C. Kendall, (ed.) Advances in cognitive - behavioural research and therapy. New York: Academic Press.

Neimeyer, R.A.. (1987). An orientation to personal construct therapy. In R.A. & J.G. Neimeyer, (eds). Personal construct therapy casebook. New York: Springer.

Noyes, R. (1981). Treatment of cancer pain. Psychosomatic Medicine, 43, 57-70.

O'Connell, W.E. (1975). Action therapy and Adlerian theory. Chicago: Alfred Adler Institute.

O'Connell, W. (1981). The natural high therapist: God's favourite monkey. Voices , 16 , 37-44.

Pancheri, P., Bellatera, M., Matteoli, S., Cristofari, M., Pollizzi, C. & Puletti, N. (1978). Infarct as a stress agent. Journal of Human Stress, 4, 41-42.

Parkes, C.M. (1971). Psychosocial transitions: A field for study. Social Science and Medicine , 5, 101-115.

Parkes, C.M. (1972). Bereavement: Studies of grief in adult life London: Tavistock Institute of Human Relations.

Pasewark, R.A. & Albers, D.A. (1972). Crisis intervention: Theory in search of a program. Social Work , 17 , 170-177.

Peck, C.L. (1984). Controlling chronic pain: A self help guide. Sydney: Fontana/Collins.

Perry, S. & Jacobsen, P. (1986). Neuropsychiatric manifestations of AIDS-spectrum disorders. Hospital and Community Psychiatry, 37, 135-142.

Peterson, C. & Raps, C.S. (1984). Helplessness and hospitalization: More remarks. Journal of Personality and Social Psychology, 46, 82-83.

Peterson, C. & Seligman, M.E. (1987). Explanatory style and illness. Journal of Personality, 55, 237-265.

Peyrot, M. & McMurray, J.F. (1985). Psychosocial factors in diabetes control: Adjustment of insulin-treated adults. Psychosomatic Medicine, 47, 542-547.

Piaget, J. (1930). The child's conception of physical causality. New York: Harcourt Brace & Co.

Pickett, C. & Clum, G. A. (1982). Comparative treatment strategies and their interaction with locus of control in the reduction of post-surgical pain and anxiety. Journal of Consulting and Clinical Psychology, 50, 439-441.

Plumb, M.M. & Holland, J. (1977). Comparative studies of psychological adjustments in patients with advanced cancer. I. Self-reported depressive symptoms. Psychosomatic Medicine , 39 , 264-275.

Plutchik, R., Jerrett, I., Karasu, T.B. & Skodol, A. (1979). Appearance of new symptoms in hospitalized patients: An instance of institutional iatrogenesis? Journal of Clinical Psychiatry , 27, 276-279.

Polivy, J. (1977). Psychological effects of mastectomy on a woman's feminine self-concept. Journal of Nervous and Mental Disease , 164 , 77-87.

Popper, K.R. (1959). The logic of scientific discovery . New York: Basic Books.

Porritt, D. (1979). Social support in crisis: Quantity or quality? Social Science and Medicine , 13 A , 715-721.

Pratt, L. (1976). Family structure and effective health behaviour : The energized family . Boston: Houghton Mifflin.

Pritchard, M.J. (1981). Temporal reliability of a questionnaire measuring psychological response. Journal of Psychosomatic Research , 25 , 63-66.

Proctor, H. (1985). A construct approach to family therapy. In E. Button (ed.) Personal construct theory and mental illness. Beckenham: Croom Helm.

Prohaska, T.R., Keller, M.L., Leventhal, E. A. & Leventhal,H. (1987). Impact of symptoms and ageing attributions on emotions and coping. Health Psychology, 6, 495-514.

Radley, A.R. (1974). The effect of role enactment upon construed alternatives. British Journal of Medical Psychology, 47, 313-320.

Radley, A.R. & Green, R. (1985). Styles of adjustment to coronary graft surgery. Social Science and Medicine, 20 , 461-472.

Radley, A.R. & Green, R. (1986). Bearing illness: Study of couples where the husband awaits coronary graft surgery. Social Science and Medicine, 23, 577-585.

Rahe, R.H. & Arthur, R.J. (1968). Life change patterns surrounding illness experience. Journal of Psychosomatic Research, 11, 341-345.

Rahe, R.H. & Arthur, R.J. (1978). Life change and illness studies: Past history and future directions. Journal of Human Stress , 4 , 3-15.

Rainy, L.C. (1985). Cancer couselling by telephone help line: The UCLA Psychosocial Cancer Counselling Line. Public Health Reports, 100, 308-315.

Raps, C.S., Peterson,C., Jonas, M. & Seligman, M.E.P. (1982). Patient behaviour in hospitals: Helplessness, reactance or both? Journal of Personality and Social Psychology, 42, 1036-1041.

Reeder, L.Q. (1973). Stress and cardiovascular health: An international cooperative study - I. Social Science and Medicine, 7, 573-584.

Reichman, S. (1981). The physician-patient relationship: Expectations and reality. Bulletin of the New York Academy of Medicine, 57, 1-12.

Reiss, D. (1981). The family's construction of reality. Cambridge: Harvard University Press.

Rimm, D.C. & Masters, J.C. (1979). Behaviour therapy. New York: Academic Press.

Rodda, B.E., Miller, M.C. & Bruhn, J.G. (1971). Prediction of anxiety and depression patterns among coronary patients using a Markov process analysis. Behavioural Science, 16, 482-289.

Rodin, G. & Voshart, K. (1986). Depression in the medically ill: An overview. American Journal of Psychiatry, 143, 696-704.

Rogers, C.R. (1987). Some thoughts. In W.R. Coulson, & C.R. Rogers, (eds.), Man and the science of man. Colombus, Ohio: Charles E. Merrill

Rolland, J.S. (1987). Chronic illness and the life cycle: A conceptual framework. Family Process, 26, 203-221.

Rosenbaum, E.H. (1975). Living with cancer. New York: Praeger.

Rosenthal, R.R. (1976). Experimenter effects in behavioural research. New York: Appleton/Century/Crofts.

Roud, P.C. (1986-87). Psychosocial variables associated with the exceptional survival of patients with advanced malignant disease. International Journal of Psychiatry in Medicine, 16, 113-122.

Rowe, D. (1978). The experience of depression. Chichester: Wiley.

Rowe, D. (1981). The construction of life and death . New York: Wiley.

Rowe, D. (1987). Beyond fear. London: Fontana.

Rudestam, K.E. (1980). Methods of self change . Belmont, California: Brooks/Cole.

Rychlak, J.F. (1988). The psychology of rigourous humanism. New York: New York University Press.

Sachar, E.J. (1975). Evaluating depression in the medical patient. In J.J. Strain, & S. Grossman, (eds.), Psychological care of the medically ill . New York: Appleton-Century-Crofts.

Sanders, J.B. & Kardinal, C.G. (1977). Adaptive coping mechanisms in adult acute leukaemia patients in remission. Journal of American Medical Association , 127, , 952-954.

Saper, B. (1987). Humour as psychotherapy: Is it good or bad for the client? Professional Psychology: Research and Practice, 18, 360-367.

Sartre, J.P. (1962). Imagination . Ann Arbor: University of Michigan Press.

Scarr, S. (1985). Constructing psychology: Making facts and fables for our times. American Psychologist, 40, 499-512.

Schar, M., Reeder, L.G. & Dirkens, J.M. (1973). Stress and cardiovascular health: An international cooperative study - II. The male population of a factory at Zurich. Social Science and Medicine , 7 , 585-603.

Schleifer, S.J., Keller, S.E., Mamerino, M et al., (1983). Suppression of lymphocite stimulation following bereavement. Journal of the American Medical Association, 250, 374-377.

Schmale, A.H. (1972). Giving up as a final common pathway to changes in health. Advances in Psychosomatic Medicine, 8, 20-40.

Schmale, A.H. & Iker, H.P. (1971). Hopelessness as a predictor of cervical cancer. Social Science and Medicine, 5, 95-100.

Schmitt, F.E. & Wooldridge, P.J. (1973). Psychological preparation of surgical patients. Nursing Research, 22, 108-116.

Schütz, A. (1976). The phenomenology of the social world. Chicago: Northwestern University Press.

Seidler, G.H. (1985). Psychosocial processing of disease exemplified by multiple sclerosis: Results of an empirical study of 27 males. Zietschrift fur Psychosomatisch Medicin Psychoanalytisch, 31, 61-80.

Seligman, M.E.P. & Garber, J. (eds.) (1980). Human helplessness: Theory and applications. New York: Academic Press.

Shadish, W.R., Hickman, D. & Arrick, M.C. (1981). Psychological symptoms of spinal cord injury patients: Emotional distress as a function of time and locus of control. Journal of Consulting and Clinical Psychology, 49, 297.

Shapiro, A.P. (1978). Behavioural and environmental aspects of hypertension. Journal of Human Stress, 4, 9-17.

276

Shapiro, D.H. (1980). _Meditation: Self-regulatory strategies and altered states of consciousness_. New York: Aldine.

Shearn, M.A. & Fireman, B.H. (1985). Stress management and mutual support groups in rheumatoid arthritis. _Amercan Journal of Medicine_, _78_, 771-775.

Shlien, J.M. (1965). Phenomenology and personality. In J.M. Wepman, & R.W. Heine, (eds.), _Concepts of personality_. Chicago: Aldine.

Shontz, F.C. (1975). _The psychological aspects of physical illness and disability_. New York: Macmillan.

Shontz, F.C. (1977). Physical disability and personality: Theory and recent research. In R.P. Marinelli, & A.E.D. Ortro, (eds.), _The psychological and social impact of physical disability_. New York: Springer.

Shorr, S.E. (1972). _Psychoimagination therapy_. New York: Intercontinental Medical Book Corporation.

Siegler, M. (1981). Searching for moral certainty in medicine: A proposal for a new model of the doctor-patient encounter. _Bulletin of the New York Academy of Medicine_, _57_, 56-69.

Siegrist, J.S. & Halhuber, M.J. (eds.) (1981). _Myocardial infarction and psychosocial risks_. New York: Springer Verlag.

Silver, P.S., Auerbach, S.M., Vishniavsky, N. & Kaplowitz, L.G. (1986). Psychological facotors in recurrent genital herpes infection: Stress, coping style, social support, emotional dysfunction and symptom recurrence. Journal of Psychosomatic Research, 30, 163-171.

Silver, R.L. & Wortman, C.B. (1980). Coping with undesirable life events. In J. Garber, & M.E.P. Seligman, (eds.), Human helplessness: Theory and applications. New York: Academic Press.

Silverman, S. (1985). Psychoanalytic observations on vulnerability to physical disease. Journal of the American Academy of Psychoanalists, 13, 295-315.

Simon, J.I. (1971). Emotional aspects of physical disability. The American Journal of Occupational Therapy, 25, 408-410.

Simonton, O.C., Matthews-Simonton, S. & Creighton, J. (1978). Getting well again. Los Angeles: Tarcher.

Singer, J.L. & Pope, K.S. (1978). The power of human imagination. New methods in psychotherapy. New York: Plenum.

Skelton, M. & Dominian, J. (1973). Psychological stress in wives of patients with myocardial infarction. British Medical Journal, 258, 101-103.

Skenazy, J.A. & Bigler, E.D. (1985). Psychological adjustment and neuropsychological performance in diabetic patients. Journal of Clinical Psychology, 41, 391-396.

Smith, E. M., Redman, R., Burns T.L. & Sagert, K.M. (1985). Perceptions of social support among patients with recently diagnosed breast, endometrial and ovarian cancer: An exploratory study. Journal of Psychosocial Oncology, 3, 65-81.

Sontag, S. (1977). Illness and metaphor. London: Allen Lowe.

Spiegel, D., Bloom, J.R. & Yalom, I. (1981). Group support for patients with metastatic cancer. Archives of General Psychiatry, 38, 527-533.

Spiegelberg, H. (1969). The phenomenological movement: A historical introduction. The Hague: Nijhoff.

Spiegelberg, H. (1970). On some human uses of phenomenology. In F.J. Smith, (ed.), Phenomenology in perspective . The Hague: Nijhoff.

Stavraky, K.M. (1978). Psychological factors in the outcome of human cancer. Journal of Psychosomatic Research , 12 , 251-259.

Stocksmeier, V. (1976). Medical and psychological aspects of coronary heart disease. In V. Stocksmeier, (ed.), Psychological approaches to the rehabilitation of coronary patients . New York: Springer Verlag.

Stotland, E. (1969). The psychology of hope . San Francisco: Jossey Bass .

Straus, A.L. (1975). Chronic illness and the quality of life . Saint Louis: Mosby.

Strosahl, K.D. & Ascough, J.C. (1981). Clinical uses of mental imagery: Experimental foundations, theoretical misconceptions and research issues. Psychological Bulletin , 89 , 422-438.

Suls, J. & Mullen, B. (1981). Life events, perceived control and illness: The role of illness. Journal of Human Stress , 7 , 30-34.

Sveback, S. (1974). A theory of sense of humour. Scandinavian Journal of Psychology , 15 , 99-107.

Szasz, T.S. & Hollender, M.H. (1956). A contribution to the philosophy of medicine: The basic models of the doctor-patient relationship. Archives of Internal Medicine , 97 , 585-592.

Tanck, R.H. & Robbins, P.R. (1979). Assertiveness, locus of control and coping behaviours used to diminish tension. Journal of Personality Assessment , 43 , 396-400.

Tarrier, N & Maguire, P. (1984). Treatment of psychological distress following mastecromy: An initial report. Behaviour Research and Therapy, 22, 81-84.

Tasto, D.L. & Skjei, E.W. (1979). Spare the couch: Self change for self-improvement . Englewood Cliffs, N.J.: Prentice Hall.

Taylor, S.E. (1979). Hospital patient behaviour: Reactance, helplessness or control. Journal of Social Issues , 35 , 156-184.

Taylor, S.E., Lichtman, R.R. & Wood, J.O. (1984). Attributions, beliefs about control and adjustment to breast cancer. Journal of Personality and Social Psychology, 46, 489-502.

Temoshek, L., Heller, B.W., Sagebiel, R.W., Blois, M.S., Sweet, D.M., Di Clemente, R.J. & Gold, M.L. (1985). The relationship of psychosocial factors to prognostic indicators in cutaneous malignant melanoma. Journal of Psychosomatic Research, 29, 139-153.

Theorell, T. & Rahe, R.H. (1971). Psychosocial factors and myocardial infarction. An inpatient study in Sweden. Journal of Psychosomatic Research, 15, 25-34.

Thomas, J.M. & Weiner, E.A. (1974). Psychological differences among groups of critically ill hospitalized patients, non-critically ill patients and well controls. Journal of Consulting and Clinical Psychology, 42, 274-279.

Thompson, S.C. (1981). Will it hurt if I can control it? A complex answer to a simple question. Psychological Bulletin, 90, 89-101.

Thurer, S., Levine, F. & Thurer, R.T. (1980-81). The psychodynamic impact of coronary bypass surgery. International Journal of Psychiatry in Medicine, 10, 273-290.

Tucker, P. (1987). Psychosocial problems among adult burn victims. Burns, 13, 7-14.

Turk, D.C. & Genest, M. (1979). Regulation of pain: The application of cognitive and behavioural techniques for prevention and remediation. In P.C. Kendall, & S.D. Hollon, (eds.), Cognitive-behavioural interventions. New York: Academic Press.

Turk, D.C., Meichenbaum, D. & Genest, M. (1983). Pain and behavioural medicine: A cognitive-behavioural perspective. New York: Guilford.

Turk, D.C. & Rennert, K. (1981). Pain and the terminally ill cancer patient. In H.J. Sobel (ed.). Behaviour therapy in terminal care: A humanistic approach. New York: Ballinger.

Udelaman, H.D. & Udelaman, D.L. (1983). Current explorations in psychoimmuology. American Journal of Psychotherapy, 37, 210-221.

Unger, R.K. (1983). Through the looking glass: No wonderland yet! (The reciprocal relationship between methodology and modes of reality). Psychology of Women Quarterly, , 8, 9-32.

Vachon, M.L.S., Lyall, W.A.L., Rogers, J. et al. (1982). The effectiveness of psychococial support during post-surgical treatment of breast cancer. International Journal of Psychiatiric Medicine, 11, 365-372.

Vandenberg, J.H. (1980). The psychology of the sick bed. New York: Humanities Press.

Vernon, D.T.A. & Bigelow, D.A. (1974). Effect of information about a potentially stressful situation on response to stress impact. Journal of Personality and Social Psychology, 29, 50-59.

Viney, L.L. (1972). Reactions to frustration in chronically disabled patients. Journal of Clinical Psychology, 28, 164-165.

Viney, L.L. (1976). The concept of crisis: A tool for clinical psychologists. Bulletin of the British Psychological Society , 29, 387-395.

Viney, L.L. (1980). Transitions . Sydney: Cassel.

Viney, L.L. (1981a). Experimenting with experience: A psychotherapeutic case study. Psychotherapy: Research, theory and practice , 18 , 271-278.

Viney, L.L. (1981b). Content analysis: A research tool for community psychologists. American Journal of Community Psychology , 9 , 269-281.

Viney, L.L. (1983a). Concerns about death in severely ill people. Death Education , 7, 229-239.

Viney, L.L. (1983b). Experiencing chronic illness: A personal construct commentary. In J. Adams Webber, & J.C. Mancuso, (eds.), Applications of personal construct psychology . London: Academic Press.

Viney, L.L. (1983c). The assessment of psychological states through content analysis of verbal communications. Psychological Bulletin, 96, 942-963.

Viney, L.L. (1984). Loss of life and bodily integrity: Two different sources of threat for people that are ill. Omega , 15, 207-222.

Viney, L.L. (1985). The bereavement process: A new approach. Bereavement Care, 4, 27-32.

283

Viney, L.L. (1986a). Physical illness: A guidebook for the kingdom of the sick. In E. Button, (ed.) Personal constuct theory and mental health. Beckenham: Croom Helm.

Viney, L.L. (1986b). Positive emotion in the physically ill. Journal of Psychosomatic Research, 30, 9-27.

Viney, L.L. (1987a). A sociophenomenological approaach to lifespan development complementing Erikson's psychodynamic approach. Human Development, 30, 125-136.

Viney, L.L. (1987b). Data collection in the social sciences: A personal construct analysis. In F. Fransella, & L. Thomas, (eds.) Experimenting with personal construct psychology. London: Routledge & Kegan Paul.

Viney, L.L. (1987c). Interpreting the interpreters: Towards a science of construing people. Florida: Krieger.

Viney, L.L. (1987d). Psychotherapy in a case of physical illness. In R.A. & G.J. Neimeyer, (eds.) A casebook for personal construct theory. New York: Plenum.

Viney, L.L. (in pressa). A constructivist model of psychological reactions to illness and injury. In G.J. & R.A. Neimeyer, (eds.) Advances in personal construct psychology. New York: JAI Press.

Viney, L.L. (in pressb). The construing widow: Dislocation and adaptation in bereavement. Psychotherapy Patient.

Viney, L.L. (in pressc). Which data collection methods are appropriate for a constructivist psychology? International Journal of Personal Construct Psychology.

Viney, L.L. & Benjamin, Y.N. (In press). Evaluation of a hospital-based counselling service. Advances in Behavioural Medicine.

Viney, L.L., Benjamin, Y.N., Clarke, A.M. & Bunn, T.A. (1985). Sex differences in the psychological reactions of medical and surgical patients to crisis intervention counselling: Sauce for the goose may not be sauce for the gander. Social Science and Medicine, 20, 1199-1205.

Viney, L.L, Benjamin, Y.N. & Preston, C. (In pressa). An evaluation of personal construct therapy for the elderly. British Journal of Medical Psychology.

Viney, L.L, Benjamin, Y.N. & Preston, C. (In pressb). Constructivist family therapy for the elderly. Journal of Family Psychology.

Viney, L.L, Benjamin, Y.N. & Preston, C. (In pressc). Mourning and reminiscence: Parallel therapeutic experiences for the elderly. International Journal of Ageing and Human Development.

Viney, L.L, Benjamin, Y.N. & Preston, C. (In pressd). Personal construct therapy for the elderly. International Journal of Cognitive Psychotherapy.

Viney, L.L, Benjamin, Y.N. & Preston, C. (In presse). Promoting independence in the elderly: The role of psychological, social and physical constraints. Clinical Gerontologist.

Viney, L.L., Clarke, A.M. & Benjamin, Y.N. (1986). A general systems approach to the patient, hospital staff, family and community: Implications for health care services. Behavioural Science, 31, 239-253.

Viney, L.L., Clarke, A.M., Bunn, T.A. & Benjamin, Y.N. (1985a). An evaluation of three crisis intervention programmes for general hospital patients. British Journal of Medical Psychology, 58, 75-86.

Viney, L.L., Clarke, A.M., Bunn, T.A. & Benjamin, Y.N. (1985b). Crisis intervention counselling: An evaluation of long-term and short-term effects. Journal of Counselling Psychology, 32, 29-39.

Viney, L.L., Clarke, A.M., Bunn, T.A. & Benjamin, Y.N. (1985c). The effects of a hospital-based counselling service on the physical recovery of surgical and medical patients. General Hospital Psychiatry, 7, 294-301.

Viney, L.L., Clarke, A.M., Bunn, T.A. & Teoh, H.Y. (1985). Crisis intervention counselling in a general hospital: Development and multifaceted evaluation of a health service. Sydney: Australian Studies in Health Care Administration, No.5.

Viney, L.L., Henry, R.M., Walker, B. & Crooks, L. (1987). Is postive emotion in patients with AIDS antibodies a defense? International Congress on Psychosomatic Medicine, Sydney.

Viney, L.L., Henry, R.M., Walker, B. & Crooks, L. (in press). The emotional reactions of HIV antibody positive men. British Journal of Medical Psychology.

Viney, L.L. & Manton, M. (1973). Sampling verbal behaviour in Australia: The Gottschalk-Gleser content analysis scales. Australian Journal of Psychology, 25, 45-55.

Viney, L.L. & Westbrook, M.T. (1976). Cognitive anxiety: A method of content analysis for verbal samples. Journal of Personality Assessment, 40, 140-150.

Viney, L.L. & Westbrook, M.T. (1979). Sociality: A content analysis for verbalizations. Social Behaviour and Personality, 7, 129-137.

Viney, L.L. & Westbrook, M.T. (1981a). Psychological reactions to chronic illness-related disability as a function of its severity and type. Journal of Psychosomatic Research, 25, 513-523.

Viney, L.L. & Westbrook, M.T. (1981b). Measuring patients' experienced quality of life: The application of content analysis scales in health care. Community Health Studies, 5, 45-52.

Viney, L.L. & Westbrook, M.T. (1982a). Coping with chronic illness: Biographic disability and handicap factors. Journal of Psychosomatic Research, 26, 595-605.

Viney, L.L. & Westbrook, M.T. (1982b). Patterns of anxiety in the chronically ill. British Journal of Medical Psychology, 55, 87-95.

Viney, L.L. & Westbrook, M.T. (1982c). Psychological reactions to chronic illness: Do they predict rehabilitation? Journal of Applied Rehabilitation Counselling, 13, 38-44.

Viney, L.L. & Westbrook, M.T. (1984). Coping with chronic illness: Strategy preferences, changes over time and related psychological reactions. Journal of Chronic Diseases, 106, 1-14.

Viney, L.L. & Westbrook, M.T. (1985). Patterns of psychological reactions to asthma in children. Journal of Abnormal Child Psychology, 13, 477-489.

Viney, L.L. & Westbrook, M.T. (1986). Psychological states in patients with diabetes mellitus. In L.A. Gottschalk, F. Lolas, & L.L. Viney, (eds.) Content analysis of verbal behaviour in clinical medicine. Berlin: Springer Verlag.

Visotsky, H.M., Hamburg, D.A., Goss, M.E. & Libovits, B.Z. (1961). Coping behaviour under extreme stress. Archives of General Psychiatry, 5, 27-52.

Viswanathan, R. & Vizner, T. (1984). The experience of myocardial infarction as a threat to one's personal adequacy. General Hospital Psychiatry, 6, 83-89.

Volicer, B.J. (1978). Hospital stress and patient reports of pain and physical status. Journal of Human Stress, 4, 28-37.

Wallston, B.S., Wallston, K.A., Kaplan, D.K. & Maides, S.A. (1976). Development and validation of the health locus of control (HLC) scale. Journal of Consulting and Clinical Psychology, 44, 580-585.

Warner, R. (1976-77). The relationship between language and disease concepts. International Journal of Psychiatry in Medicine, 7, 57-68.

Watson, M., Greer, S., Young, J., Inayat, Q. Burgess, C. & Robertson, B. (1988). Development of a questionnaire measure of adjustment to cancer. Psychological Medicine, 18, 203-209.

Weaver, R. (1973). The old wise woman . New York: Putnam.

Weinberger, M., Hiner, S.L. & Tierney, W.M. (1986). Improving functional status in arthritis: The effect of social support. Social Science and Medicine, 23, 899-904.

Weiner, B. (1985). "Spontaneous" causal thinking. Psychological Bulletin, 97, 74-84.

Weisman, A.D. (1972). On dying and denying . New York: Behavioural Publications.

Weisman, A.D. & Kastenbaum, R. (1968). The psychological autopsy : A study of the terminal phase of life . New York: Behavioural Publications.

Weisman, A.D. & Sobel, H.J. (1979). Coping with cancer through self-instruction: A hypothesis. Journal of Human Stress , 5 , 3-8.

Weisman, A.D. & Worden, J.W. (1975). Psychosocial analysis of cancer deaths. Omega , 6 , 61-75.

Weisman, A.D. & Worden, J.W. (1976-77). The existensial plight in cancer: Significance of the first 100 days. International Journal of Psychiatry in Medicine , 7 , 1-15.

Weiss, S.M. (1969). Psychosomatic aspects of symptom patterns among major surgery patients. Journal of Psychosomatic Research , 1969, 13 , 109-112.

Wellisch, D.K. (1981). Intervention with the cancer patient. In C.K. Prokop, & L.A. Bradley, (eds.), Medical psychology. New York: Academic Press.

Wellisch, D.K., Fawzy, F.I. & Yagger, J. (1978). Life in a Venus-Flytrap: Psychiatric liason to patients undergoing bone marrow transplantations. In R.A. Faguet, F.I. Fawzy, D.K. Wellisch, & R.O. Pasnau, (eds.), Contemporary models in liason psychiatry. New York: Spectrum Publications.

Wellisch, D.K., Mosher, M.B. & Van Scoy, C. (1978). Management of family emotion stress: Family group therapy in a private oncology practice. International Journal of Group Psychotherapy, 28, 225-231.

Westbrook, M.T. (1976). Positive affect: A method of content analysis for verbal samples. Journal of Consulting and Clinical Psychology, 44, 715-719.

Westbrook, M.T. & Viney, L.L. (1977). The application of content analysis scales to life stress research. Australian Psychologist, 12, 157-166.

Westbrook, M.T. & Viney, L.L. (1980). Scales of origin and pawn perception using content analysis of speech. Journal of Personality Assessment, 44, 157-166.

Westbrook, M.T. & Viney, L.L. (1981). Biographic and illness-related predictors of patients' reactions to the onset of chronic illness. Advances in Behavioural Medicine, 1, 57-74.

Westbrook, M.T. & Viney, L.L. (1982). Psychological reaction to the onset of chronic illness. Social Science and Medicine , 16 , 899-905.

Westbrook, M.T. & Viney, L.L. (1983). Reactions to illness of men and women across the adult life span. Journal of Health and Social Behaviour, 24, 313-324.

Wiklund, I., Sanne, H., Vedin, A. & Wilhelmsson, C. (1984). Psychosocial outcome one year after a first myocardial infarction. Journal of Psychosomatic Research, 28, 309-321.

Williams, G.H. & Wood, P.H. (1986). Common sense beliefs about illness: A mediating role for the doctor. The Lancet, Dec. 20/27, 1435-1437.

Wolpe, J. (1973). The practice of behaviour therapy . Oxford: Pergamon.

Woodfield, R.L. & Viney, L.L. (1985). A personal construct approach to bereavement. Omega , 16, 1-13.

Woods, N.F. (1975). Human sexuality in health and illness . St. Louis: Mosby.

Worden, J.W. & Sobel, H.J. (1978). Ego strength and psychosocial adaption to cancer. Psychosomatic Medicine , 40 , 585-591.

Worden, J.W. & Worden, A.D. (1984). Preventive psychosocial intervention with newly diagnosed cancer patients. General Hospital Psychiatry, 6, 243-249.